The Jim Richardson Boat Book

An Ocean World Publication

The Jim Richardson Boat Book

From Interviews with

JAMES B. RICHARDSON
Master Shipwright of the Chesapeake

Edited by ROBERT C. KEITH

Illustrated by ELLEN CORDDRY

Published by Ocean World Publishing Co., Inc.
Baltimore, Maryland 21231

Library of Congress Catalog Card Number: 85-62579
ISBN 0-9609772-2-8
Printed in U.S.A. by BookCrafters, Inc.
Type: 11/13 Palatino, by EPS Group, Baltimore

Editor's Preface

This book grew out of a series of conversations and taping sessions at Jim Richardson's home near Cambridge, Md., from 1980 through 1984. Jim saw the popular Rien Poorvliet-Wil Hsuygen *Gnomes* book one day and figured the story of building a boat could be told the same way—heavily illustrated, with a loose and informal editorial structure. My role has been to help organize the material and try to make sure everything is clear, even to those, including longtime sailors like myself, who may be clumsy with tools and a bit mystified about how sailing craft really work.

The book has been a joy to transcribe and edit. Jim remains a captivating figure at age 78. "There's a man and a half," observed a woman many times his junior after one brief meeting. His gift for story telling—the pace, the cadence, the humerous twist—shines though the technical explanations, so that the book can be enjoyed and appreciated at several levels. It is a book for anyone who likes boats and water and things made of wood. But it contains insights (and provocations) which will fascinate the expert. And it can be used as a guide by someone bold enough to actually undertake the construction of a large wooden sailing ship.

The book also contains some American oral history. For example, it includes Jim's detailed explanation of the dying art of building from a carved wooden model. The advantages of this technique will be seen from the book.

* * *

Since he was a small child, Jim Richardson has lived a few miles west of Cambridge on a family tract overlooking LeCompte Bay, a small tidal inlet off the lower Choptank River. Appropriately, Jim's house, which he started to build in 1935 (and has never really finished) stands on the site of an old shipyard, one operated by a family named Hermes before the Civil War. Jim found the remains of the sawpit when he laid the foundation for his porch.

This part of Maryland's Eastern Shore is one of the few culturally distinctive areas left in America. As soon as you sail from Jim's place into the river, you are looking directly upon the scene of James Michener's *Chesapeake*. Michener spent many hours with Jim in researching the book. And when, in *Chesapeake*, you come across the fiercely individualistic, extremely devout Paxmore boat-building family, you identify instantly. Jim seem to walk right out of the book.

Jim's roots in America go back more than 300 years. His mother was a LeCompte, descended from a French Huguenot family that arrived on the inlet in 1650. His boatbuilding antecedents on his father's side go back nearly as far. The first Richardsons opened a boatyard sometime in the late 1600s, in the vicinity of what is now called Federal Hill in Baltimore. "We don't know whether we are Scotch or English," Jim says. "I asked my grandfather about it one time and he said, "They lived pretty close to the line. They always fought on whatever side they thought might win." Jim adds, "Judging from the height of the men in the family, there might be a little Nordic mixed up in it."

The Richardsons eventually moved to the Eastern Shore for better access to timber near the water. At least half the men have followed the water, or stayed in water-related business, up to the present generation.

Although Jim's grandfather worked in as shipyard, his father did not. He was a millwright. "He tried building a few skipjacks but found it an unprofitable venture," Jim says. As a boy Jim spent some time as a carpenter in local shipyards, but prior to World War II he mainly did other kinds of woodworking around Cambridge in association with Oscar Seward, another local man. Jim opened his boatyard after the war, as he says, "for reasons I'll never know." His father's assessment of the business proved correct. Jim has been given many placques and awards, including the title "Admiral of the Chesapeake Bay" bestowed upon him by Maryland Governor Harry Hughes in Chesapeake Appreciation Days ceremonies at Sandy Point in 1979. But honors and recognition are not edible, and for Jim, as for many artists and artisans who give something special and extra to their work, the rewards have been personal rather than financial.

Jim's love of boats is exceeded only by his love of people, who fascinate him no end. The feeling is reciprocated by a stream of Sunday visitors who treasure his company. Friends and admirers find him courtly, courteous, considerate, humble, generous, and a wonderful, patient teacher. At the same time he can be outspoken, impish and at times deliberately and outrageously provocative. He thrives on conversation, and is not averse to throwing on a little gasoline whenever it begins to flicker.

He is strongly religous. When his father became an Adventist in the early 1900s, his mother "went along with it," and Jim, his wife Generva, and two married daughters follow the faith today. The Richardsons had three children, but tragically, a son, Jimmy, was lost to the water, killed by lightning in 1948, at age 13, while sailing near home in the log canoe *Flying Cloud*. Jim's sons-in-law attempted to carry on the yard business, but eventually their building and rigging talents led them to surer employment at maritime museums.

—Robert C. Keith

THE SEA GYPSY

There's a schooner in the offing,
With her topsails shot with fire,
And my heart has gone aboard her
For the Islands of Desire.

—Richard Hovey

Contents

Author's Introduction

We're doing this book in the hope that it will be of interest to a novice, or to folk that have some interest in a thing of this kind, and not to be so technical that we could be criticized by technical folk.

I don't know whether I have the grace that Mr. Chapelle* had. Mrs. Chapelle came around to where Mr. Chapelle and I were visiting one day and she was shaking this magazine. I knew she was very irritated and so did he, but he stopped to light his pipe, and then he looked up and recognized her, and she says, "Chappie, have you seen this awful thing this man wrote about you?"

He says, "Yes, Zama, I saw it."

She says, "Well surely you're going to have them do a rebuttal."

He drew a long draw on his pipe and blew the smoke, drew another one and blew the smoke, and he says, "Heavens no, I've been criticized by *experts!*" Then he says, "Jim, what were we talking about?"

Well, I don't know if I have that kind of grace or not.

* * *

In this book I refer to the boat-builder as "he," so some people will criticize me for that. Well, I suppose that there's an awful lot of women who own their own boats, but I don't know of any that ever started one keel up. Not that it couldn't be done. My two sisters are stone masons, although they're non-conformists as far as following the rules are concerned. Eastern Shoremen are notorious for being non-conformist.

I have had a number of young women help me in the yard. Several became very accomplished with the adze, and two others turned out much of the business for the *Dove* on the lathe—blocks, deadeyes, trunnels, belaying pins and that sort of thing. Marilyn Reilly was a big help to me on the *Jenny Norman.*

* * *

The first boat I ever built for myself was exactly like a hog trough. Whenever I put it over it would leak. It lasted one season. Later on I shared a workbench with my father. I had him with me till he was in his 90s. Even then he would come by two or three times a week, scan what I was doing, and cough. That cough always meant you were headed for disaster. He was a good instructor. My family has seen me through the *Jenny Norman*. I couldn't have gotten her afloat without my brother Bill. There are thousands of people I'd like to thank. Everybody has been so good to me.

—J. R.

---

*The late Howard I. Chapelle was transportation curator of the Smithsonian Institution and author of several classic books on American small craft and boatbuilding.

Some definitions...

Just so no readers will be confused by unfamiliar terms, I should explain right here what some of the parts of a boat are called, and what functions they serve.

The *keel* is the big long thick piece of wood at the bottom that everything attaches to. It is the backbone of the boat, it's strongest part. At the forward end of the boat—the *bow*—you have a big piece called the *stem,* which comes up from the keel at an angle. At the after end—the *stern*—you have another large piece called the *sternpost.* To that you generally attach another large piece called the *horn timber.* All the rest of the boat is built around these major pieces.

Under the keel, you have some kind of fin to keep the boat from slipping sideways when you are sailing close to the wind. This fin could be a deep, heavy extension of the keel, or if your boat is intended for shallow waters, it could be a *centerboard* which pivots down through a slot in the keel and is housed in a watertight *well* or *trunk* which runs lengthwise down the middle of the boat. You raise and lower the board with a rope as needed: down to help hold your course to windward, up to travel over shallow bottom, or to reduce drag when you are are sailing off the wind.

Coming up from the keel, you have ribs, called *frames,* which determine the shape of the boat. The ribs are covered by *planking,* and of course across the top you have *decking.* The rear of the boat can be shaped in any of several ways. In most cases you have a squared-off section called a *transom.* Alternatively you could have a *round-stern* boat, or you could have a *double-ender,* which comes to a point at each end like a canoe.

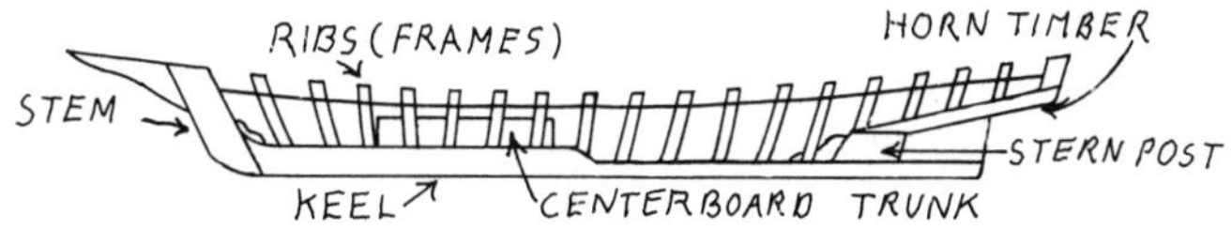

HOW LONG IS A BOAT?

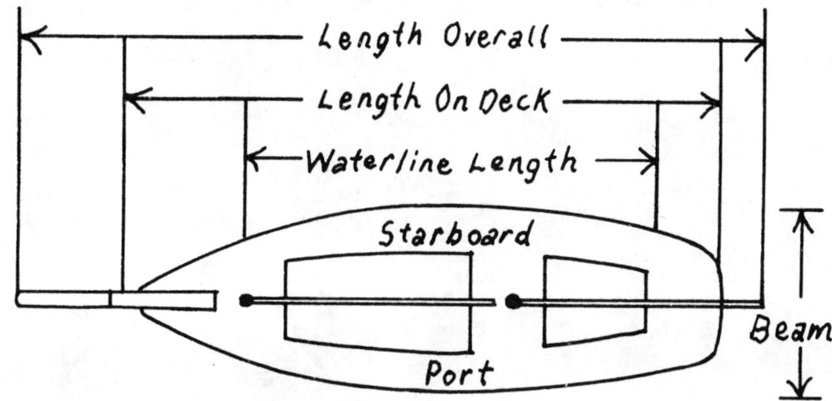

In addition to the parts of a boat, you have a number of areas with special names—the *bilge,* which is the lowest area, under the floorboards, the *cabin,* where you cook and sleep, the *cockpit,* where everybody sits in the sun while you steer the boat. The *rudder* is the piece that actually controls the direction of the boat. You operate it with a *wheel* or *tiller,* and you have to stay with it, stay at the *helm,* as they say, just as you have to stay with it when you are at the wheel of a car.

The width of a boat is called the *beam,* and its depth in the water is called the *draft.* And of course the right side is *starboard* and the left is *port.* When you get all that straight in your mind you can begin to see how a boat comes together.

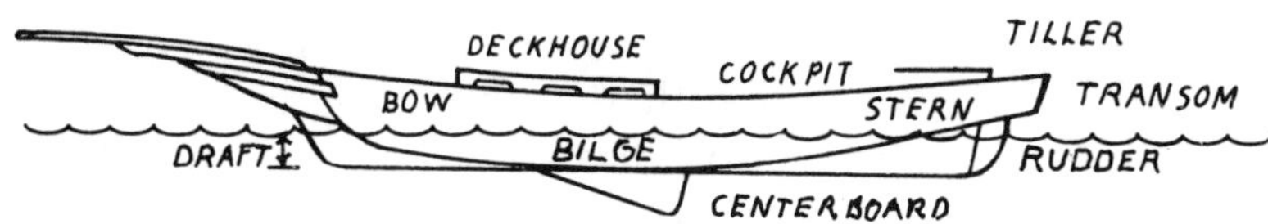

Chapter I:

Begin with a Dream

Every boat begins with a dream.

There you are in bed with your feet sticking out of the bottom of the covers and dreaming about all these boats going by. After awhile, you will settle on the very one, and it will be standing there in bright lights.

Then you begin to study, talk to people, look at other boats like it. You will want the most practical, easiest handling design for the work and the money and the length and the width and everything that goes into it.

A good boat will get you from here to there and provide a safe and comfortable place to live in transit. It will get you off the highways and on to the water and under the sky. It will let you live your dream.

The way I go about it, you begin your boat by carving a solid wooden model. Unless you are trying to invent something, you use a successful earlier hull as your inspiration. For my bugeye, the *Jenny Norman,* I used the lines of a 78-footer and scaled everything down so as to have a 48-foot boat which should work just as successfully for her size.

After making your model, you go out and look for parts. Rather than going to a log yard or a sawmill it would be better to find a standing tree at least for several of the big pieces. If you're a ribbon clerk or something like that and not familiar with the area you'd have problems finding what you want but it would be worth the looking. Once you find the parts there would have to be some time devoted to the prepping of them. The keel would surely have to be chopped by hand. There's only one straight line—that's the very bottom of it where the *worm shoe* goes. All the rest of the lines are coming and going.

If you are doing a centerboard boat, you would cut the slot for the centerboard, through the keel, and put the *logs* in to make the centerboard well. You would fasten on the stem and sternpost. You'd be ready then to get the setup for the ribs—making them and hanging them. The method I use is to take the dimensions off my wooden model. We'll get to that later on. I don't think it will be too complicated but I don't know how to do it in a few words.

Once you begin to get the ribs, then you put the deck pieces in—we're talking now about the fore and aft pieces, the *knees* if any—all that kind of mess. Then you plank, and after you've got the planking, then you deck. By the time you get to the deck you've got the better part of it behind you. Or maybe I should say worse part, because so much of it is working against gravity, especially the under planking. Sometimes you can turn the boat over to do your planking but in a big boat that can be more complicated than working on your back in the sawdust.

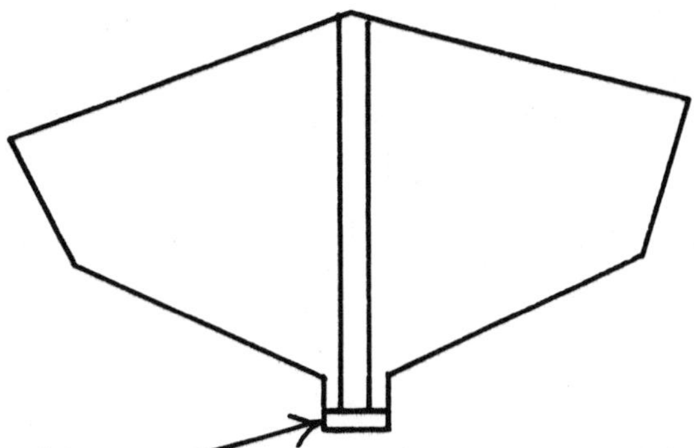

Worm Shoe – It's the first thing they eat, and is relatively easy to replace. Shipworms, also called toredoes or marine borers, are not really worms but soft little crustaceans – sort of like clams without shells – that feed on wood. They are the ultimate menace to a wooden boat because they eat holes through it if you let them. You find them only in salt water mainly in the spring of the year.

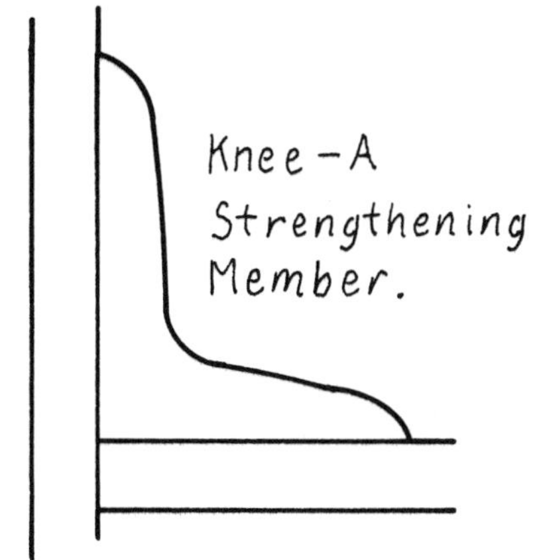

You wouldn't go into *spar*-making until the decks were on. But as the decks were laid, and probably before you finish the deck house, you might work the spars and the house along in conjunction with each other. On the *Jenny Norman* I had to rough saw my spars sooner to save them because I had them around for so long. If I didn't take care of them I would have lost the pieces from rot. I couldn't afford that.

Just a word of caution. The actual *building* of a boat is not exactly a thing to run after. If anybody is going into it for the pleasure they would get out of the work on it, they would be someone who had not earned their livelihood in a boat yard. Anybody in his right mind who wanted a boat would by all means hire it built rather than do it himself if money were no object. I certainly wouldn't struggle over the *Norman* if I could hire help. Everybody says I love to do it but that's because they don't know what they are talking about.

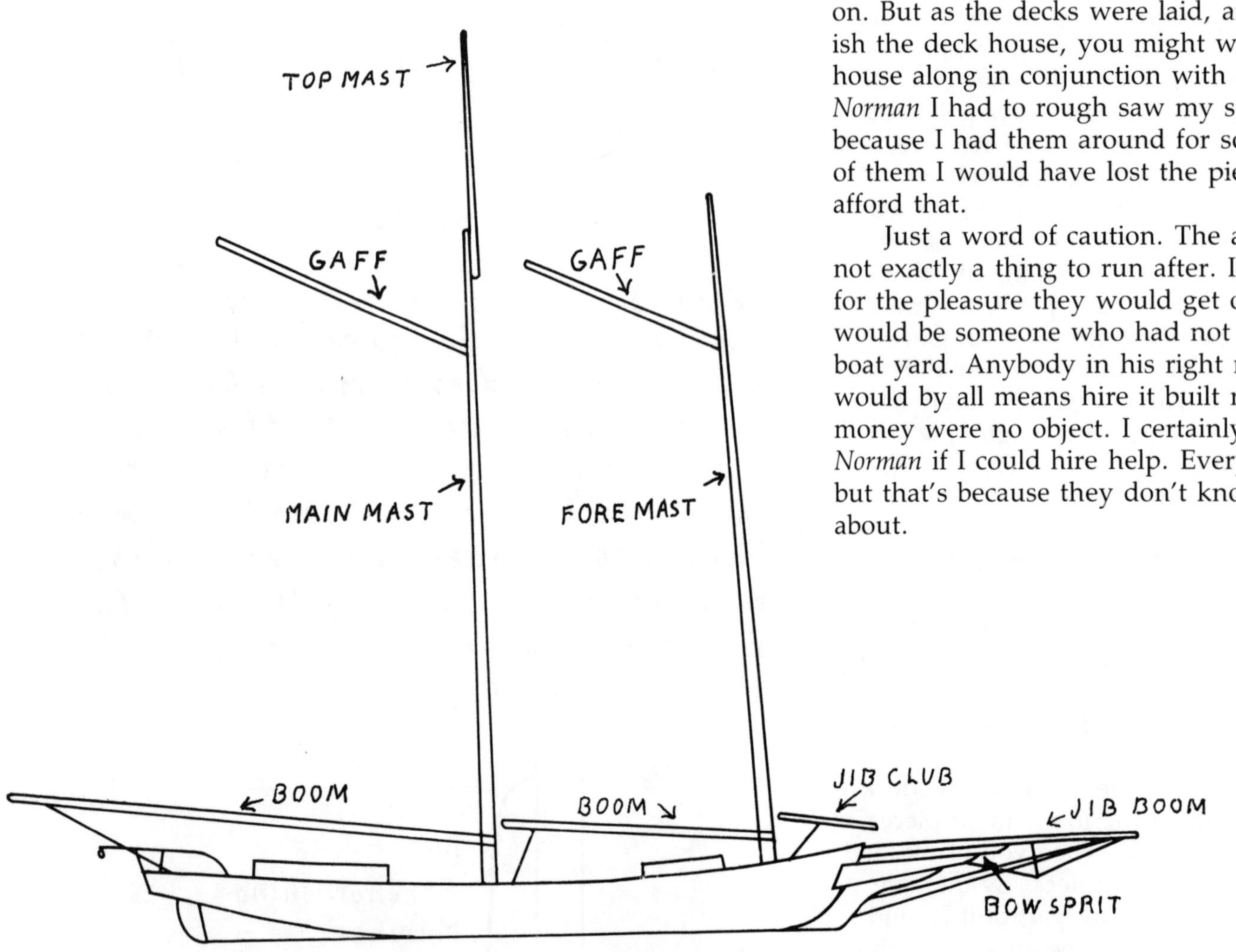

SPARS ON A SCHOONER

SPARS - Refers generally to masts, booms and the like.

Q. *Can a novice really expect to build a successful large boat?*

A novice who has a feel for his tools and an eye for fair lines can build anything that he has a mind to, out of wood. All he's got to do is keep himself properly informed, and there's plenty printed for that. Also he has to be sure not to rush out poorly advised and buy impossible lumber. But if he has the time and is acquainted with the use of hand tools, he can set himself up and build any boat up to a point—something under 50 feet. He can work with mechanical aids like a boom built on the back of some light truck for lifting and placement. It would take several years. If we're talking about a schooner that would be used as a pleasure yacht he could settle himself in for four or five years.

We know a lot of people who start a boat while they are working so as to have it ready when they retire. That's a good plan, but your wife and family have to have an unusual attitude toward your project. She'll want to go to the beach in the summertime just as sure as fate, and half your weekends will be taken up by whatever if she doesn't have an interest of her own that would necessarily be hers and not have to include her husband.

I was up at Marblehead one time and the men were all sitting under the stern of a boat drinking beer and the women were sanding the daylights out of the sides of her. I thought to myself, if I don't move up here I've lost my mind. But then they told me how deep the snow had been that winter and I said no, I'd rather be where I am and let Mother do the cooking and stuffing and everything while I sandpaper.

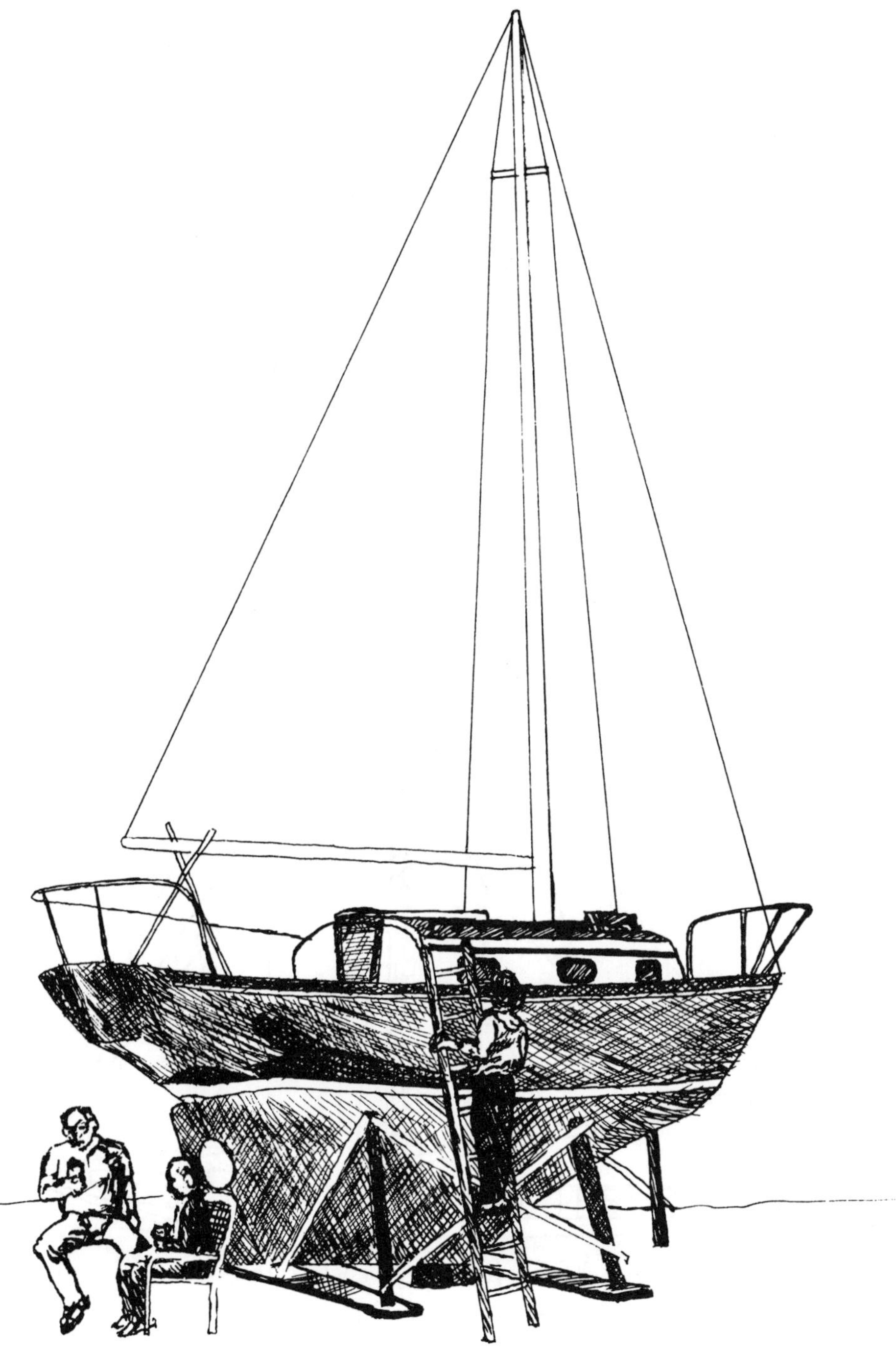

Chapter 2

Choosing the Sail Plan

CHESAPEAKE BAY SLOOP
NONE ARE LEFT

During my whole lifetime, since I was a teenager, I wanted a sloop. When I say sloop, I'm not talking about what they call nowadays a sloop. So far as we are concerned here on the Bay, a sloop is a gaff-rigged boat, with a heavy built little hull, very full bow, beautiful lines, wide, round bilge, with a centerboard. She had her *gaff mainsail*, a *topsail*, *jib*, and *flying jib* which ran from the end of the bowsprit to the top of the topmast.They were built on Taylor's Island and there were many on the Bay.

I had gone to the Smithsonian and picked up what they said were the lines of the *William Wesley*, and they were near enough. They would have made a nice little sloop. I hadn't seen the *William Wesley* out of the water, and certainly I hadn't measured her, but I had sat on her deck and dreamed a many a time eating sandwiches for lunch. I wanted a sloop like that all my life and when it came near time for me to retire I talked to Cook Todd, who had the last sloop on the Bay with its working rig in it. He used to come here to the railway to get his work done.

I told him I wanted to build one of those things when I retire, which wasn't going to be too long.

He said, "What for?"

I said, "Sailing around in."

He said, "You can't have one of these things for sailing around in."

I said, "What's the matter, why can't I?

He said, "Because you gotta have four people with you to get her underway."

I said, "Explain it."

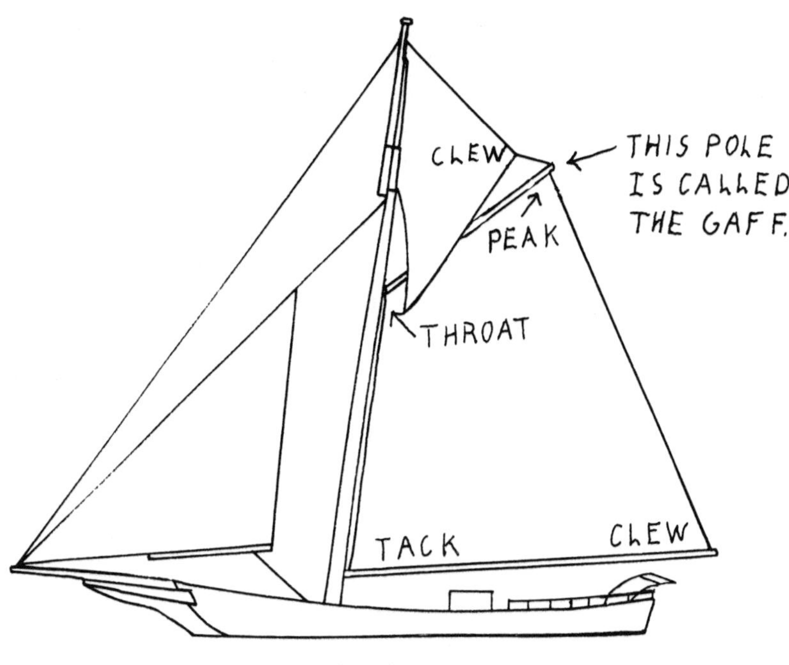

GAFF RIG

The mainsail is rectangular, and throat and peak are raised by separate ropes.

JIB-HEADED RIG

The mainsail is a triangle. Another name for it on Chesapeake Bay is "leg o'mutton" sail, because of its proportions.

He said, "If you have two people, and you both get on the *throat,* then you can't *peak* it. And if you peak it, then you can't throat it." Their *gaff* and their sail was all so heavy. And he said, "You've got to have a *jib-headed rig,* like a bugeye, if you're going to sail it alone.

And it was just the same as hitting me in the head with a baseball bat. I knew *immediately* that he was a hundred percent right.

---

*Yachtsmen would call a triangular sail marconi, but marconi suggests a tall, very efficient, very thin sail, not a workboat sail. Take an 80-meter racer: a 45-50 foot boat, 8-10 feet wide with a 50-60 foot mast and a 12 foot boom. That's the most efficient sail you can get, a long thin wing up there. The shorter the boom, the more efficient it is so far as going into the wind and that sort of thing. But, by the same token, you lose power all the time you shorten the boom. You certainly couldn't dredge with an 8 meter.

When you choose your sail plan, you have to think to yourself, "What can I handle alone," because, otherwise, you'd be like Mr. Morrison, even if you have sons growing up. He got his boat, and he only used it a year or two before the boys wouldn't go with him because he didn't have television aboard. If he didn't have television they couldn't see the football game.

So, if you plan to go sailing when *you* want to go sailing, and if it's not going to be a straight out motor boat which you can go in anytime, then you don't want to have to round up four or five people every time to go with you. You've got to have a single-hander.

Now, how large a boat can you single hand? That has lots to do with the rig. I built a little boat for some people that was only 32 feet and the best I remember she had seven or nine sets of halyards on her foremast. She was designed by one of our most prolific marine designers. The people took it to the Bahamas where they wanted to go. They came back and sold it immediately on their return and have never had a boat since.

KETCH

You can have a boat with a simple rig that will handle a lot easier and be a lot more pleasure than some smaller boats with running back stays and all kinds of strange combinations of sails, nine halyards on the foremast and all.

I had a cousin named Turkey Marshall and he sailed a 60-foot bugeye all of his adult life alone. In fact, he did it with only one leg. He had lost a leg from an injury, so he just hopped around to handle the boat. So, in choosing the *Jenny Norman,* I knew that I could handle 48 feet if I had anything like decent help.

Now it's not a question of having as *few* sails as possible. Some people will see a boat with one mast and one large mainsail and they might think, that should be fairly simple to manage, and then they will see a boat with two masts and several sails and they think that looks complicated or difficult. Of course it's just the opposite. You can see with the sloop I wanted to do, at 40 feet of length it would have had a 40-foot boom on it and a 20-foot gaff to pull up, and the gaff would have been at least six inches through its heaviest girth. We're talking about quite some-

SCHOONER WITH BERMUDA RIG

thing in that sail as it begins to come up. You begin to get tremendous weight.

In a jibheaded rig you don't get any weight until you've about got the sail up, but even a jib-headed sail can be difficult to manage on a boat much over 30 feet long, especially if the wind gets up and you have to take her down and reef her. So what you do is split the rig—divide it—so that you have two masts and two smaller sails. That way when the wind is light you put everything up, and if it starts to blow hard you just drop one of the big sails and continue on your way.

If you are thinking about the very easiest rig going into something with a little bit of size—35 feet, 40 feet, even 32 feet—and you are ruling out the yacht per se, the honest-to-goodness racing machine yacht—the easiest thing to handle would be a split jib-headed rig...a *ketch* or *Bermuda* rig or something like that.

The only reason you would go into a gaff-rigged schooner, instead of a jib-headed design, would be that they are a lots prettier boat, and you can get more sail on them, and then when you don't need it you can cut the sail down without too much goings on, and still have a very able boat and rig. And if it is balanced well, if you've got it figured out well, it will sail as well as anything.

On a 40-foot schooner, the sail area would be broken up, split, and her gaff would be small and light so that two people would be able to get the sail on her, and possibly one person if he was husky. But I would think it would have to be a schooner that was a yacht type rather than a workboat type, as far as the weights of things.

The schooner would have a topsail on the main mast. I don't think this would be difficult to handle. You set it or take it in all from the deck. It stays up there in a bundle. The only time it would need some attention would be when you leave it for a long time without getting it properly aired, because it won't shed water 100 percent when you clew it up with a clew line.

GAFF-RIGGED MAIN TOPMAST SCHOONER

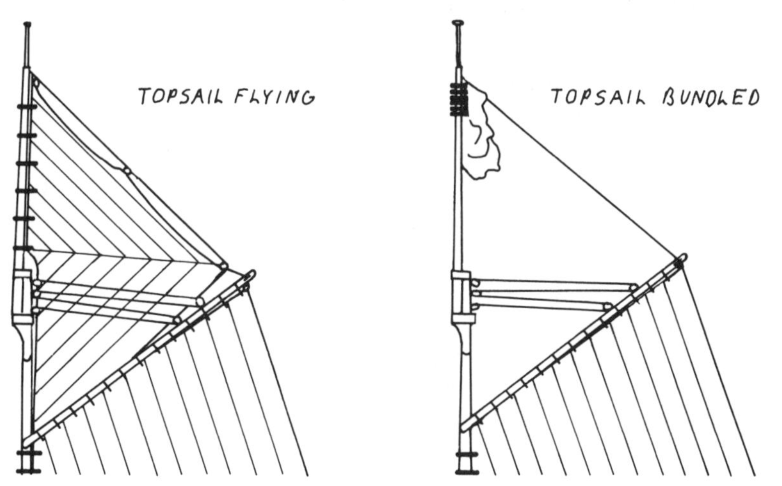

Q. When you work out the sail plan, do you start with so many square feet for the size of the boat?

You start with making a mistake or two, and as that cautions you, then you get smart, or get out of business. But yes, you try to figure out what you're going to do. If you are going to do a three-sail bateau—that's like a skipjack but with divided rig—then you've got to get that square feet of canvas worked out into a balanced three sails. Just the same when you are doing a bugeye or schooner rig. You've got to put on as much sail as you'd have on a single-masted boat but you've got to get it worked out into the three sails and see if you can get them something into balance. You have to have some little bit of feel for what is balanced.

Q. When you speak of balance, what do you mean?

Well, you can have a boat where you have to brace your feet on the collar and pull your arms out of joint to keep her on course, holding her rudder over 10-15 degrees, whenever a breeze hits her. By the same token you can have one that's light-headed so that every time a wind hits her she will go down wind. That's the most dangerous rig you can have because when she heads down like that you can't get her back up.

So when you think about a balanced sail rig you're thinking about a rig that does come up when a wind hits her but she doesn't jump right up into the wind ready to go about if you're not sitting there pulling your arms out.

The idea in designing your boat is that the *center of effort* on the sail's part should coincide somewhat with the *center of lateral resistance* of the hull.

Now the center of lateral resistance has to do with the whole wetted surface of the hull. It is the hinge point, the point where one end of the boat isn't any easier to push around than the other end. It's like the button on the back-house door. If you don't put the nail in the center of it, it's going to hang heavy end down.

Q. How do you determine the center of lateral resistance?

Well, one of my architect friends cut a silhouette out—a piece of cardboard—and he would balance that on a thread to see where the center was. That's just great if it is a flat cardboard boat. It just so happens that it's not a flat cardboard boat, so he was just wasting his time. He'd have been better out cutting his grass.

Marine architects will go round and round trying to figure out hull displacement, center of lateral resistance, center of effort. It's more difficult on a split rig and it's also more difficult on a boat with a hard chine—that's a V-bottom boat—because the hull changes so radically as it heels over. On a round-bottom boat the hull does not change that radically.

Even when you have a designer who has figured out the weights and displacement and this and that and the other thing it's not every time that they will get a good balanced boat. I mentioned earlier this boat that had seven or nine halyards and was designed by one of the best designers here in the East, with one of the best reputations. The boat was a a total complete failure. The hull was poor and the rig was worse.

So I don't care who the designer is, unless he has searched through and found something that has been tried and proven you are not ever going to be sure until you sail her.

Q. So, how do you work out the balance on a boat?

By looking at it. If you are a novice and don't have any idea yourself you get somebody else to look at it. One time

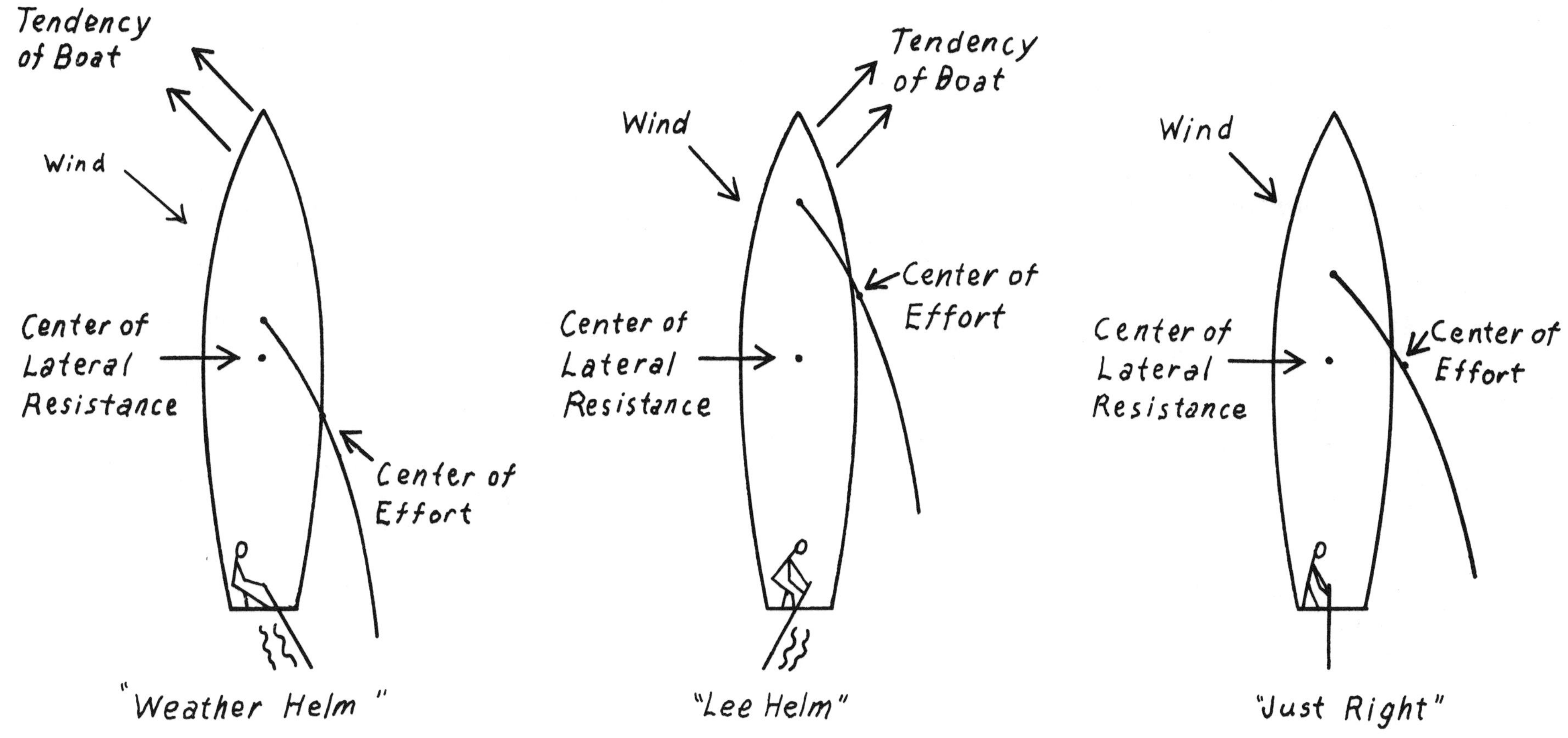
Tendency of Boat
Wind
Center of Lateral Resistance
Center of Effort
"Weather Helm"
Wind
Tendency of Boat
Center of Effort
Center of Lateral Resistance
"Lee Helm"
Wind
Center of Lateral Resistance
Center of Effort
"Just Right"

Mother and I were sitting here eating lunch and a boat came into the creek. I had seen the boat being built, but she didn't have her masts and rigging on her then, of course. When I saw it overboard I didn't recognize it. I said, no, I don't know what it is but I do know one thing, it won't sail. It was completely out of balance, terrible. The man came out here in front of the house and anchored. Next thing I knew two men were putting ashore with a sail bag. They came up here in the yard and we were still sitting at the table, so I said to him, come on in. He only wanted to bother me for a little while, how close was he to Wenona—how long would it take for him to get to Albert Brown's sail loft? I said to Mother, can you run them to Wenona? It's about 50-60 miles from here because you've got to go down to Princess Anne and turn off. Well, anyhow, Mother ran them out there and they left their sail, but I couldn't help it, I had to say to him what do you ever want to take your sail to Albert Brown for? The man said he couldn't handle the boat, she won't sail. I knew it wouldn't sail when I saw her, but it wasn't anything the sailmaker could fix. You do have to have some feel for it.

Q. Is there any rule a person can use for placing the mast?

Well, with a centerboarder you've either got to have your mast off center, fore and aft, or your centerboard off center. You can't step a mast on top of a centerboard well.

With the *Jenny Norman,* I have two masts. I thought I'd put 55 and 53 feet in her and have them fairly small. It will be an old man's Sunday sailer.

Q. Isn't there some formula for where they should go?

Uh-huh. And I'm ignoring it. It's smart to use the formula for skipjacks if you are doing just one mast. For the *Jenny Norman* I used the skipjack formula so far as the bowsprit's concerned. But I'm not going to go into that any more here because that would *really* bring it on, the criticism I mean. That's something like matrimony. You can get awfully involved in that. With our sketches I'd just as soon go ahead and step the mast in an appropriate-looking place.

Anybody that would describe what we are talking about in general terms, and then say if you put such and such in this spot, and all the sails in this spot, in feet and inches, and she'll balance, he would either be a fool or a novice. Or perhaps an architect. The late Owen Davis, he was a whiz kid and an architect, he told me if you want to get the right balance on a skipjack you should set your rig ahead about five percent of what your calculations come out. He could not rest unless he figured it out. He never did get it right, but you know what I mean. He monkeyed with it a great deal.

Q. But it is a critical decision?

It determines whether the boat will sail.

The Skipjack Formula

This is something our forebears fell upon around the turn of the century. For years it went by word of mouth:

Her mast is the length of the boat on deck plus the width.

Her boom is the length of the boat on deck.

Her bowsprit outboard beyond the stem is the same as the width.

When you get all of these things correlated it doesn't necessarily mean that you're going to have a balanced rig, because where the centerboard is placed up and down the keelson and how far aft you step the mast certainly has a bearing. But if you don't follow the formula, then you will have something other than a skipjack, particularly as to performance.

There's a so-called skipjack on the Bay now. The man who built her had never built anything before. I told him

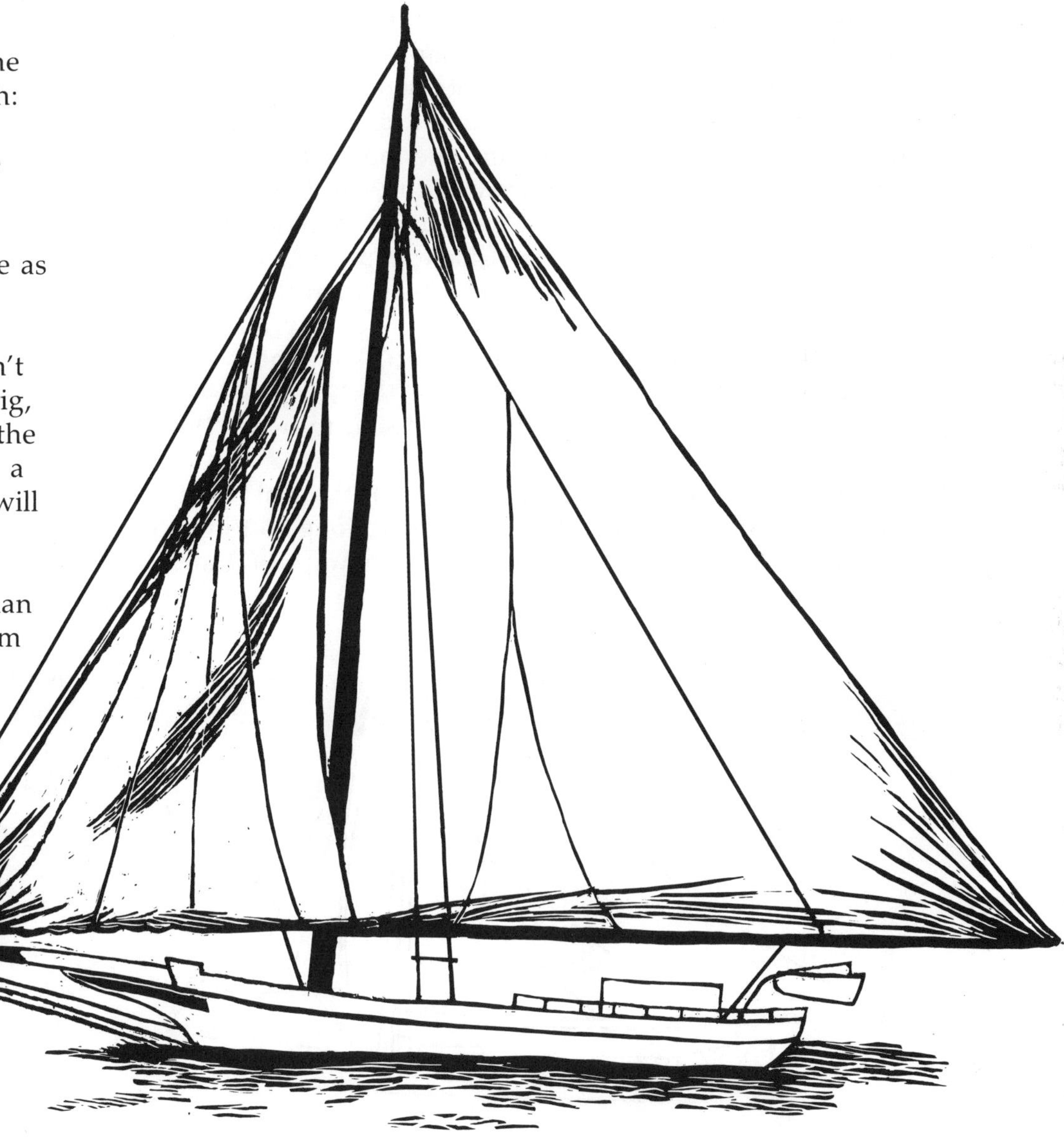

what dimensions to use and all that sort of thing.

Well, when he sailed that thing into the creek I said to my family, "For Lord's sake, what happened?" My first thought was that Mr. Speiser did not send him the length of mast I had asked him to. But I thought to myself, no, it's a man's business to sell lumber, and the longer pole he sent, the more money he'd get so he wouldn't cut it short.

So I ruled that out while I was sitting there eating. Then I thought, well, what must have happened was that his fir sides were two or three feet longer than they were supposed to be and he just used all the sides up and still put the same length of mast in her. But I knew he'd sawed the bowsprit off.

When he got up here in the yard I said to him, "What happened?

He said, "Well, my wife was afraid of the mast being that high and I didn't like the bowsprit so long so to get the same sail area I sawed the mast and the bowsprit off and added it to the boom."

That's a fact.

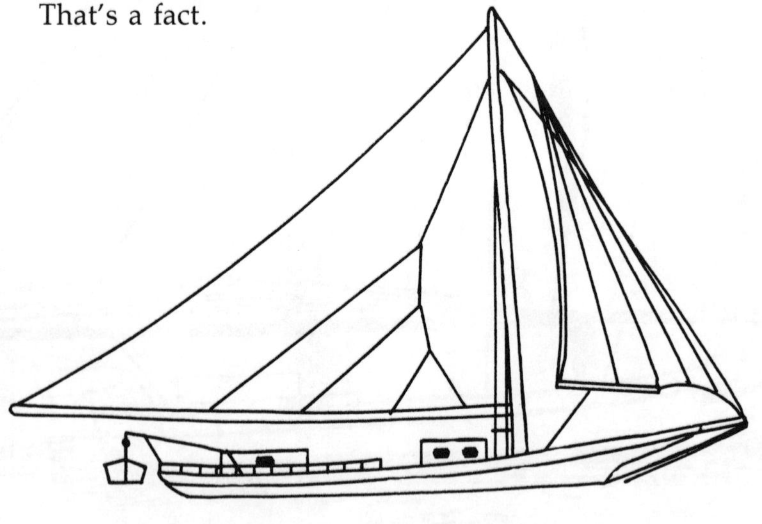

UNSKIPJACK

How MUCH Sail?

If you are going to build a Sunday sailer, a boat that's going to be used in the summer time and not very much in the winter, well, since you have mostly light airs in the summer, you can carry a bit more sail than if you are going to work her on the oyster rocks all day, every day in the winter.

That is, *unless* you have a Dr. Jones or somebody that's as old as I am stumbling about on deck, slow thinking and slow acting, then you want to cut into it a bit. Dr. Jones had a little boat built here and I put the rig on her for a boat that was at least 8-10 feet smaller than his boat was. And I though that I might have trouble with it, but the next thing knew he was bragging all up and down the Bay how stiff she was. Just so he was going, he wasn't thinking about whether somebody was passing him or not. She was able and all that with her little short rigging and he was really happy with her.

There are two ways to limit the sail area of a boat. One is to build a a short rig, as I did for Dr. Jones. The other, of course, is for the persons operating the boat to take sail off and on, and take in and shake out reefs, as they go along. But that's work.

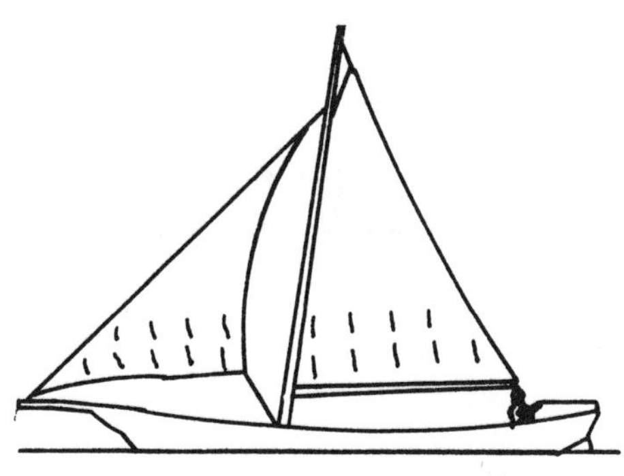

STIFF
Carrying it easy, you never have to reef the sail or anything, you go right under full sail all the time.

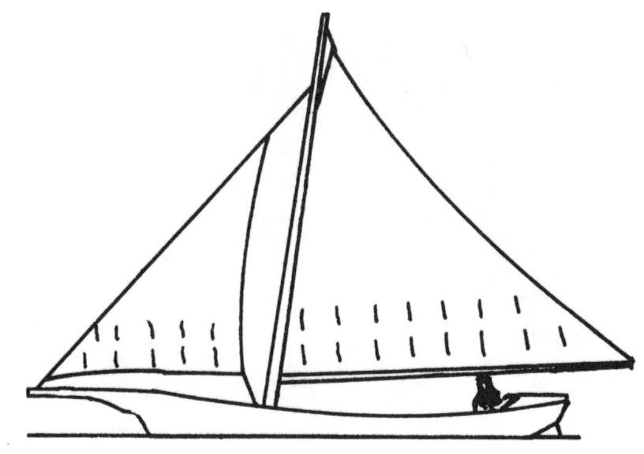

TENDER
More responsive in light airs, but she may keep you on edge when the wind gusts up, and you may want to reef.

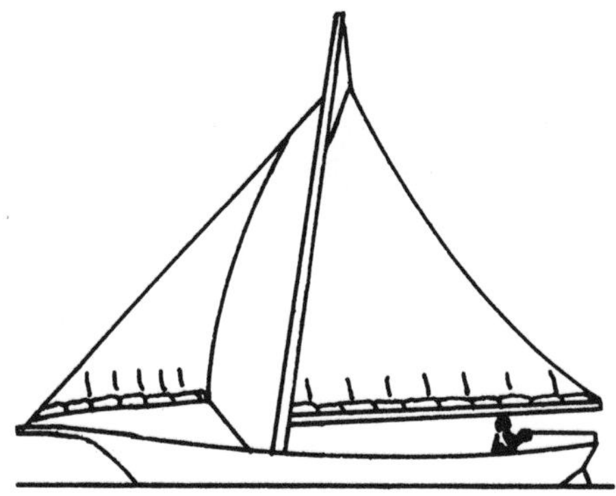

REEFED SAIL
Bottom of sail is gathered at the reef points and tied in heavy wind, thus reducing the sail area.

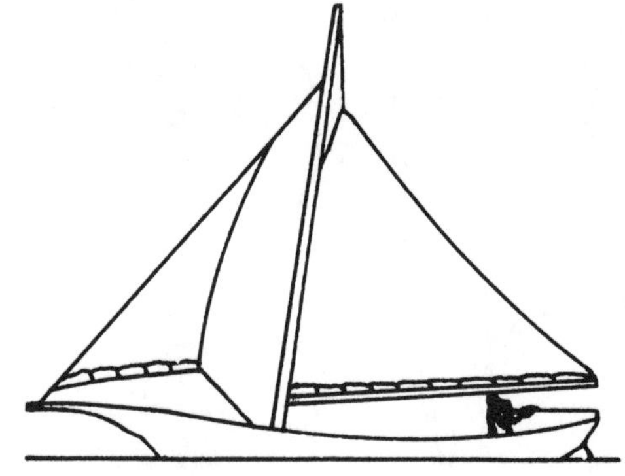

DOUBLE REEF
Some dredge boats have four reefs. This helps control speed while working the oyster beds.

Chapter 3

Making the Model

Some people are amazed to discover that there were people who built boats without blueprints, with a half model, and that the boats actually went out and lived a lifetime.

With a model, you can get something that you want, not something that somebody might want for you. Where would I go to find somebody that would ever design me a bugeye? First he'd have to look up in his printed material and see what a bugeye was, how it was built. Then he would charge as much for the plans—and rightly so—as what it would take to buy all the rough lumber. Then you would be mooning over that the rest of your life instead of going ahead with your work.

Theoretically a blueprint can save you time, in that you'll have a table of offsets—heights and widths at short intervals—and you can start out immediately with this table of offsets. You lay down all the lines and make molds—patterns—for every frame. You do this in your mold loft, and then you send the molds out to the man who is getting out the frames. He lays the mold on the timber and cuts the timber. That's what a designer wants you to do if you're going to use his blueprint. But, if you don't have a good mold loftsman, or if you don't have a lot of experience in it yourself, or don't want to take time away from the other work to fool with it, it can be a very expensive way to build.

Another problem is that a lot of designers have never built a boat. I don't suppose there's one in a hundred who has served an apprenticeship in a yard. Some of them aren't familiar with the weight of materials that are available over the counter nowadays.

We've had real famous architects that have called for 5 by 7s. There's no such a thing sold. There's 6 by 8. There's 4 by 6. It's very difficult to work from plans if the architect is not familiar with what's available in the market, because if you go to a sawmill man and ask him for a load of 5 by 7s you're going to get hurt. What we had to do on the *Dove* was get oversize and cut them back and throw away scrap. It costs a lot of money, takes a lot of time. But if you're going to have a design and don't work by it you're in trouble.

Q. When you work from a blueprint, don't you have more assurance that the design will succeed?

Certainly not if your architect is trying to design something new. And if he is not trying to design something new, he will do the same thing you would do if you are building from a wooden model. He will refer to something that's already been done—try his best to find something that was successful, and near enough to him that he could go and take the principal dimensions and such off of it and incorporate it all into what his customer is requiring. So if you would go to one and ask for a 40-foot schooner design, he would right quick look up what successful schooners there were in that category and find one that came as near as he could to what you were talking about, and he'd sit down and design it for you and it would be his design, but in reality it had a been gone over before. If your objective in building a boat yourself is to save money, and that is the only objective I know of, you can avoid this. You can do the same thing with a model.

Now, I am not proposing that anyone would work without a plan. A model *is* a plan. The only time I might work without a plan would be on a straight-sided boat like a skipjack, which I am very familiar with. On a skipjack, after you set up your keelson and your stem and your transom, the very next thing you do is bend on the side planking, just bend it in the air without frames, only a couple of braces in the middle. At that point the shape of the boat is determined. You do it by eye. From then on just follow standard procedures—nail on the bottom planking, turn her over, do the decking and so forth. A good shop man can finish the boat. But you've got to have a model when you are doing any round-bilge boat.

Q. How do you go about making a model?

Well, you don't take somebody else's model and measure it up. But just so you won't think that I'm a smartalec, I did take the lines of the original *Norma* and try to run them down to a little over half of her size for my own boat. It didn't work, but I do have some lines that were a big help to me when I was whittling my half model. I ran her down from 75 feet to 48. But it didn't work in direct proportion because it made her too low-sided. It was impossible. So I added a foot to the sides. From the *head* down to the keel my bugeye is the same as the *Norma*, run down and carried back in direct proportion. But when I added to the sides I excited my friends, because they wanted me to hold the deck to the width it would be if I had left the sides low and not let them carry out forward. Mr. Chapelle was sick over it. He didn't want me to do it. But, when I talked to the dredgers, the people that have used them, they told me to leave it alone. They said it would make her dryer.

Every marine architect that has criticized my model has said the same thing. "Why she's way too wide forward. You're not going to build her like this are you Jim?" Mr. Whitholz and George Meese and Mr. Chapelle and two or three others all criticized that model the same.

I think Mr. Chapelle thought that she wouldn't be that kind in a sea, that she would thump right sharp if I was bucking it. I figured I'd rather be dry and thumping a little bit, which I don't think she's going to do. She *is* going to have tremendous lift. You can see that when you stand smack-dab in her bow and look at her.

Q. How did you develop your eye for boats?

I might not have. We won't know unless I live to finish the *Norman* and it's successful. But what you do, what shall I say, we had to maintain these things in the boatyard all my lifetime. We were maintaining them for the oyster dredging industry. There were some that we liked and some that we didn't like, and of course we knew how they all handled. You try to accustom your thinking to the ones that were the easiest to work and were the fastest in carrying a full load under sail. So that would naturally influence one. We worked on those that were slow and able, and saw them die. We worked on those that were fast and able, and some that were neither fast nor able. I suppose that's how I came by what I thought was a combination of the best I could get in this small a boat.

Q. What can a novice do give himself confidence, some feeling that if he carves a model, then spends four or five years building his hull, that when he gets it out on the water it's going to work okay?

Alternative Method

Sometimes, in building a boat, you need to take the lines off the owner rather than some other boat. There was a very nice woman who spent her summers near the yard who was the sister of a famous Cleveland Indians baseball player. She used to bring the children she took care of over here to play with our kids' little kayaks. When she left for the winter she ordered one built for herself. Well, I took the lines off her chines—I measured her across—what else do you do when someone wants a kayak? I made the dumb thing. Come Christmas, we got a card saying she had met this wonderful man, he was so attentive, so kind, so this and that. I went down to the shop and put the kayak up on the rafters. I knew she had other things than kayaks to think about. I never heard from her again.

Of course he's got to study other hulls. If he could find a hull that suited him fine and was pretty and practical it would certainly be the surest way to come out. But if he wanted to work in a few details, then the thing to do would be to take principal dimensions and work from there, and have somebody who had had right much experience criticize it.

You could take any professional sailor—not a Sunday sailor but a skipper who had been in sail the greater part of his life, not a naval or Coast Guard man—they just killed all those people *again*—not those people but somebody that had sailed on a Cape Cod fishing schooner or something like that, and he could look at it and say uh-huh, or uh-uh. It would be no problem.

Now, it is absolutely necessary for anybody working from a half-model, or a whole model, to be acquainted with vessels enough so that they know the weight of the *scantlings* and how they are put together and that kind of thing. Scantlings covers almost everything in some architects' language. That's what you're using for frames and what have you. The whole framing of the thing is scantlings.

There's a story told about a man in Baltimore who built himself a boat—he was a carpenter, and it appeared to be a nice job, but when it came time to launch it he got his friends, some on the dock and some in the cockpit, and as they pushed it out in the water it curved right over and floated on its side. He had built it too light. Then somebody told him the best way to distribute some weight in it evenly was to pour concrete alongside the keelson. Somehow they got the boat back on the shore and poured in what looked like a likely amount of concrete. When the concrete was hard they launched it again. This time it hung heavy in the water and started leaking through the seams and the next thing they knew it was down on the bottom. I believe he just left it right there.

Now there is another man that is an artesian well expert on the other side of Baltimore who built his own skipjack and he went about it the right way. He got plans from the Smithsonian but they were only lines—they didn't have detailed sizes or descriptions of anything. He spent at least half his Sundays on the Shore one summer and he knew who was building what and what weight of materials was going in every one of those boats.

So, in doing a model, unless you have some knowledge, you'd have to ask somebody, hey, how heavy is this, or what weight of materials are we talking about for that. And if anybody was too proud, or didn't trust anybody, why he'd better buy plans and not fool around with a model. By the same token many people have been so indoctrinated that they would feel very uneasy without a set of blueprints. So to satisfy their own mind that they had what they wanted they are going to go out and pay a lot of money for a set of plans even if they do have all kinds of strange things on them.

Q. Do you prefer a half-model or a full model?

A full model gives you a whole lots better visual perspective. For the *Jenny Norman* I made a full model. With a half-model you just don't get the full benefit of the looks of the thing. However, you've got a half of the boat, you see the half, and if your mind is alert enough to put the other half in perspective then you have something easier to work with when you start building the actual boat. I'm talking about heights. It doesn't make any difference with the width. But the vertical is lots easier to get from a half-model, easier to get the rake of the deck, easier to get your heights at any point. We'll get into all that later.

Q. How do you actually make the model?

You cut a block of wood. It's going to have *sheer* in it. It's going to have *flare* in it. It's going to have a lot of things in it that if you made a heavy paper pattern it would be of no use at all to you when you go to cut the piece of wood on the band saw.

So what you do first is make sure that your block has plenty of wood in it to make your heights and widths. Then you draw your deck plan on this block of wood. You have to have pencil lines to draw the band saw to.

You should set your band saw over six or eight degrees so that you don't have to work from a dead straight up and down block. If you wanted to do that you could get your deck dimensions but you would have to work all that other wood off by hand. Better to set that band saw so that she'll give you a little bit of flare to the hull fore and aft.

In cutting at an angle around the deck lines, you have to leave extra wood, an extra quarter or five-sixteenths of an inch or whatever, to compensate for the fact that your deck is going to drop down—be lower amidships than at bow or stern—when you cut the sheer in her. Even on a model as small as the one for my bugeye—1/2 inch to the foot—you're going to drop down half an inch in the middle. It's not too difficult once you get in your head what it's going to look like.

My wife will tell you that I filed and sandpapered and chisled and whittled on that thing I've got for a whole winter and I've still got some plastic wood in it. After I had it done, a child came up here and told her that I had it lopsided.

(To page 22)

Getting Some Terms Straight

Q.What is sheer?

Sheer is the rake of the deck fore and aft.

Q. What is deadrise?

From the waterline under is deadrise. That term applies whether the hull is round, like a bugeye, or hard-chine like a skipjack. Straightbottomed Chesapeake Bay workboats are *called* deadrises, but even so, deadrise is the general term for that aspect of the boat, round or straight. I don't suppose they have any straight deadrise in Mystic, Connecticut. They hate anything that would be Chesapeake Bay.

What is flare?

That would be the contour of the bow above the waterline. I don't believe I've heard the contours of the boat defined except by portions or areas. In some vessels you have tumblehome in the middle of her.

Tumblehome?

Yes, tumblehome. Taper in from the waterline. A long time ago when they were fooling with ships they had tumblehome all the way down. That's when they were taxed by the size of their decks, and the more she tumbled home the less deck she had and the less tax you paid on her. That's why so many of the old ships were like barrels. They used the size of the deck for tax purposes, rather than carrying capacity, because it was lots easier for them to measure.

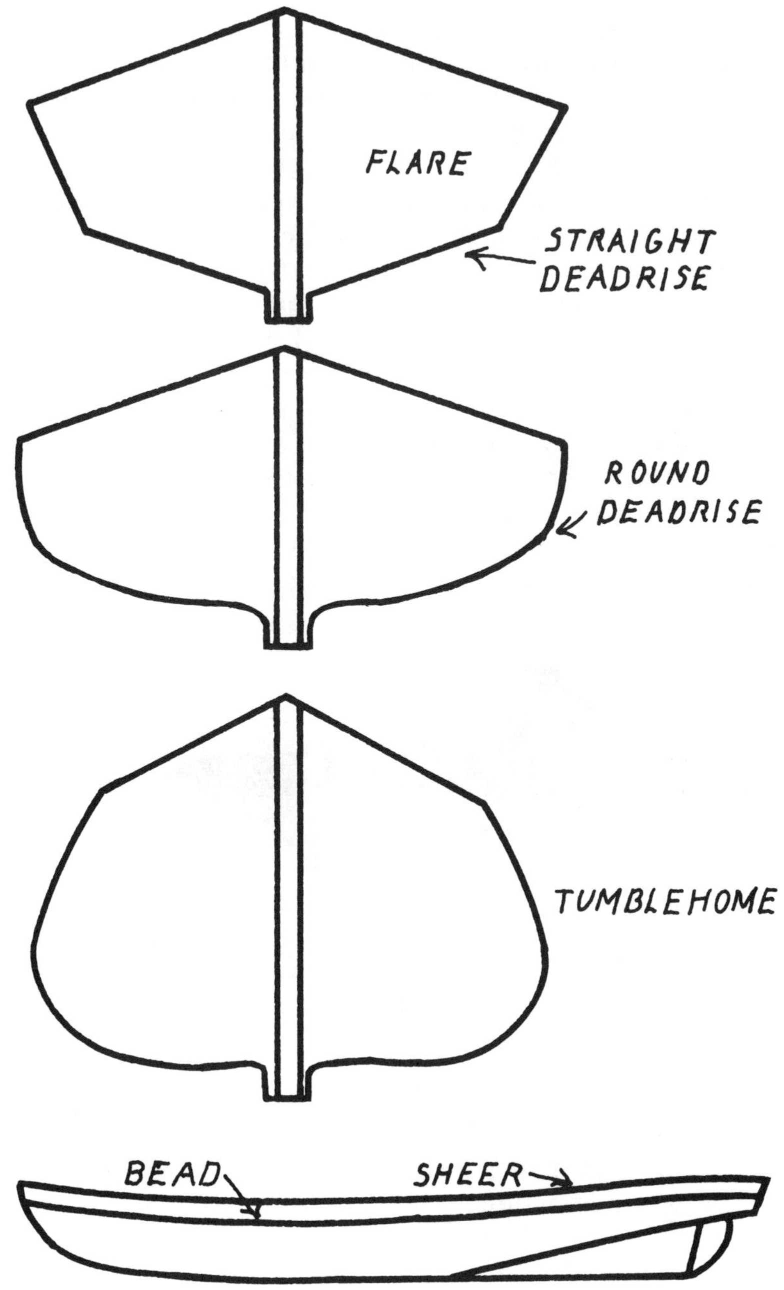

This was little Joey, who lived up the road. He was 9. He visited Mom one day and took a look at the model, as he liked to do. "I wouldn't want Mr. Richardson to know I said it but it's lopsided," he says to her.

Well, when I came home to supper she told me. I said it was not. I sat down and ate my supper and all the time I was thinking about it. As soon as the table was cleared I set it up and leveled it and started to work on it. Sure enough it had a little lump on it in the forward quarter, and it was small enough that I could sand it off. I didn't have to dress or plane it, just used coarse sandpaper and smoothed it back up again. I put it back where we kept it, and I asked Mother not to say anything to Joey.

By and by he came again and looked at it. "You know, Mrs. Richardson," he says, "when I looked at this thing last time I was here I'd have swore it was lopsided." He went on to win an award for duck carving.

Mr. Chapelle didn't want anything to do with a boat that wasn't built from blueprints and lofted. When we had *Champion Girl* swelling up in the creek, he came by with a friend from Maine. The friend went down and looked at her, and then he came back and he said, "It looks to me as if she'll sail, Howard."

"It doesn't matter if she does," Mr. Chapelle replied. "He can't build another one. He doesn't have any plans."

When we built *Sweepstakes* for him, we didn't have any trouble till we turned her right side up. "It isn't right," he said.

"What's the matter, Howard," I said, "I'll try to fix it if I can." I had been following his blueprints, so I suggested that he check the dimensions himself.

"You're not using a baseline," he said.

"I certainly am," I said. I uncovered some dirt fore and aft of the boat and showed him two steel pins I had driven into the ground. I had set them with a transit and they were exactly level. I explained that I stretched a string between these when I wanted to check dimensions. Otherwise I put the string away because you don't want all that string in your way when you are working.

"What do I do, scratch out a trench and run the string between these pins?" he asked me.

"No, Howard," I said, "You don't dig a trench. You put sticks in the ground and stretch the string between them, so that the string comes exactly two inches above the top of the steel pins."

Well, I lent him a measuring tape, and I lent him a plumb bob and I lend him this and that. He fooled around for a while and then he went to lunch. Mr. Chapelle had an allergy, and whenever he got excited or upset he got out his nasal spray. So he came back from lunch carrying this nasal spray. He fooled around some more, and finally he came up to me and said, "The hell with it," and he went home.

I had occasion to visit his home about three days later, so I asked Mrs. Chapelle if he had told her what was wrong. She said, no, he thinks there's something wrong but he can't find it. Well, I knew he couldn't find it, because the fault wasn't in the boat. It was in the blueprints.

Mother tells me I owe so much to Mr. Chapelle. I was very fond of him. He was an architect and historian, not a builder.

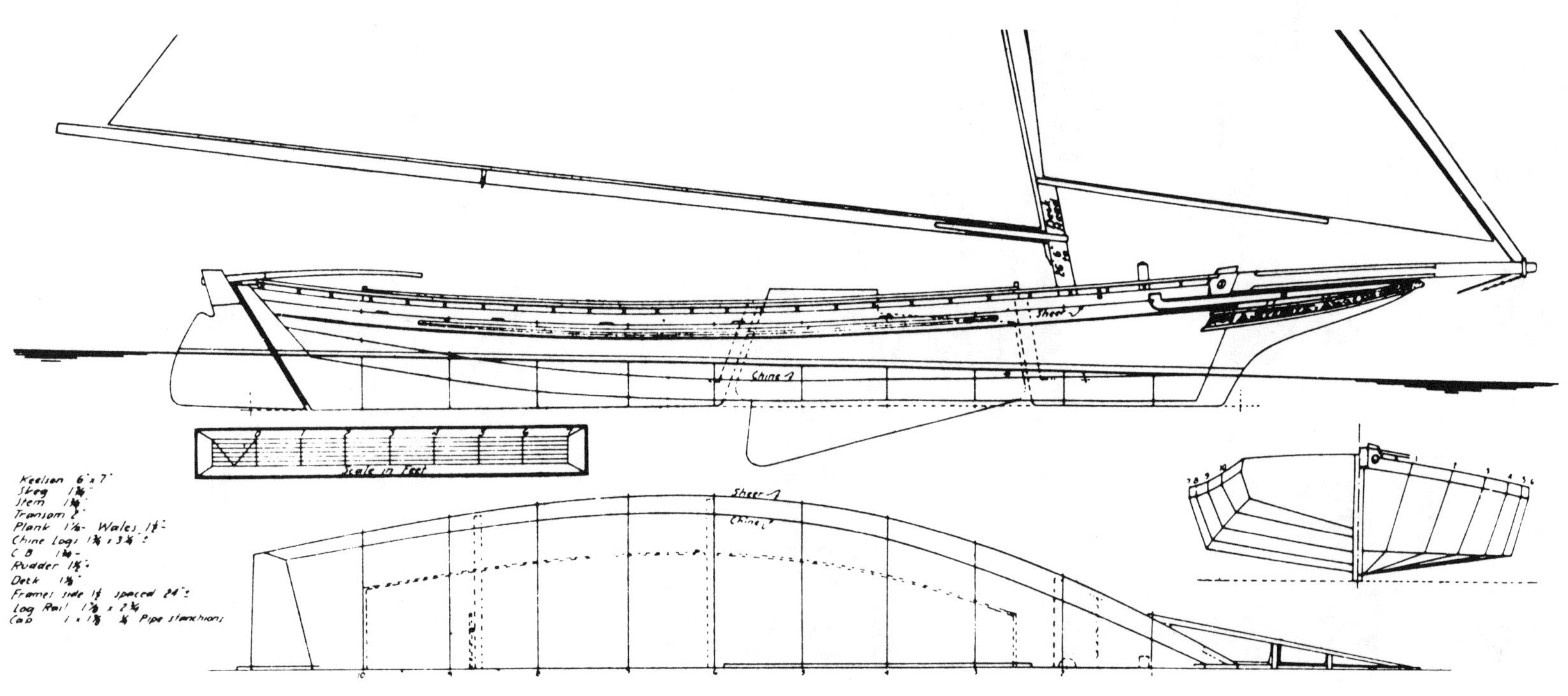

Howard Chapelle preserved the lines of many Chesapeake Bay vessels with drawings like these, now on file at the Smithsonian Institution. The lines of "Teddy", a small crab-scrape bateau, were taken in 1942, at Lower Hoopers Island. This tiny skipjack was 22'6" on deck, and drew only 14½ inches with the centerboard raised.

Chapter 4

Building the Hull

Certain parts of a boat are not standard at a lumber yard or any other place. So if you are choicy and don't want to make them up or go about it some other linty way you are best off to find a standing tree.

For instance, if you wanted an extra good knee for anchoring the stem to the keel, you would look for that in a stump and a root, or a top and a limb. The stem itself could be made from the tree.

You also might want to make the sternpost and the horn timber from a tree so it would be all in one piece. The horn timber is the part that runs from the sternpost up to the transom. The orthodox way to make the horn timber is to bring it down and bolt it across the head of the sternpost. But it's one of the weakest places in her.

You would look for your keel at a hardwood mill, somewhere they were cutting oak—making pallets or whatever. If you were on extra good terms with the man and asked him to save you a good straight piece, you would get a keel lots faster than you would by finding a standing tree and trying to negotiate with the owner of the timber to sell it to you.

You need a a good size piece, one about 30 feet long that will square up 18 inches at the narrowest end. It has to be especially large if you are going to put a centerboard through it.

A designer would feel it necessary to put in the specifications what has been put in them in all my memory—no knots, no wrens, no sap, no this and no that, but all of that is something like the lawyers do, it's just language brought over to us by custom. We don't have that kind of timber any more.

After you've located the keel and the heavy end pieces, you are ready to order your material that's going to make up the ribs. For that you want oak, for its strength.

When it comes to planking you have some choice. I know a man that is right now in the throes of building a skipjack. He has had boats all his life and is a man of means, but since everything began being so expensive he thought, seeing as how he was so knowledgeable about these things, he would just build his own boat and save that money.

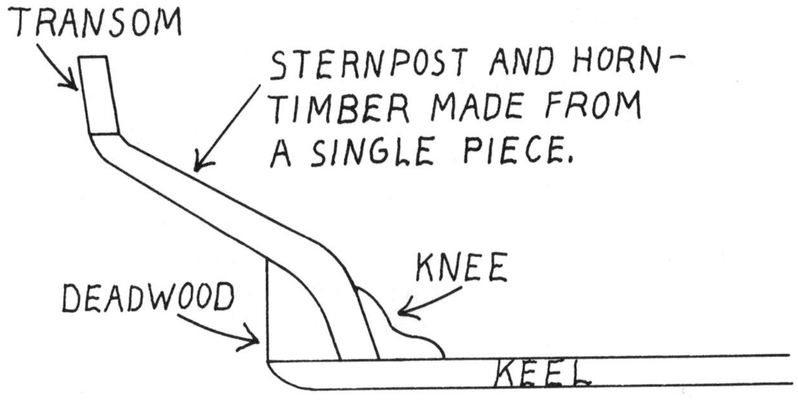

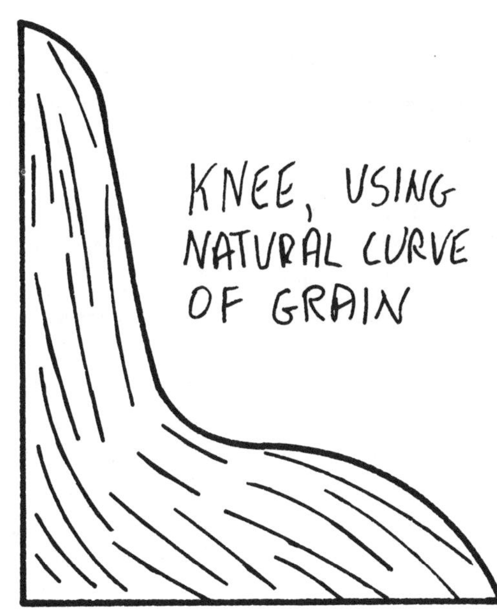

He had some sort of idea that he didn't want to use native materials so he went to a big lumber yard in Baltimore and he was conned into buying a bunch of appatan for his planking—he's talking about heavy planking, inch and a quarter thick, five inches wide.

He's been crying bitter tears ever since. He's been over here twice, and I had to turn around so he wouldn't see me smile but it's just giving him a fit. Appatan is a South American hardwood and it has interlocking grain. You can't work it either way. It won't dress. It will not plane. Your fit has to come from the saws. You saw it right and put it on. But that's impossible at times. I'm sure it will make him wonderful planking if he ever gets it on, but it's not the planking material that some of the maghoganies, or cedar or even a good grade of fir would be. Surely if you can get hold of it there's nothing that beats oak.

Q. Many people like the look and feel of a wooden boat but they worry about maintenance. What do you say about this?

Well, this depends a good deal on the owner. Boats made of the wood we have nowadays seem to be vulnerable the first years and after that, they go 25-30 years. The crucial thing is to get her over the first five years. If you can stick with her, and you have the experience, and are aware of what to take care of in those early years, then you won't have that problem anymore for the next 25 years. I don't know of any boat that I built that isn't still going.

In this area we build of wood because it is a tried and true material. We've had people that have had generations of experience in working wood. We don't have generations of people who have worked plastic or cement or metal or whatever—although I wouldn't be surprised if we did come to metal more and more in boats of some dimension. There'll always be plastic. If it hadn't been for plastic I don't think there'd have been a boat in every garage. Plastic certainly has put more people on the water.

Making the Keel

Every boat has a backbone, ribs and skin, and, of course, in building it you start with the backbone. When this backbone is outside the boat, under the frames, sticking down in the water, it's called the keel. When it's inside, more or less on top of the frames, it's called the *keelson*. The rule is pine for the keelson, oak for the keel. Oak is strong and straight, but the stump end of a pine tree can give you a nice upsweep for the after end of the boat, which you need in a keelson. The old timers used gum for the keel. It was hard and wouldn't split.

Keels are often made to go deep into the water for extra stability, so people tend to classify boats as being either keel boats *or* centerboarders. This isn't necessarily the case. With our 40-foot schooner, we'll probably plan a straight flat keel, with centerboard slot cut through it.

One of the first things to decide is where that board will go. The thing has to be placed in her according to her deadrise. If the boat is fairly flat on the bottom you can carry the board farther forward. If she has a lot of deadrise the board should step aft a foot or two. Experience and looking at them and talking with the dredgers will teach

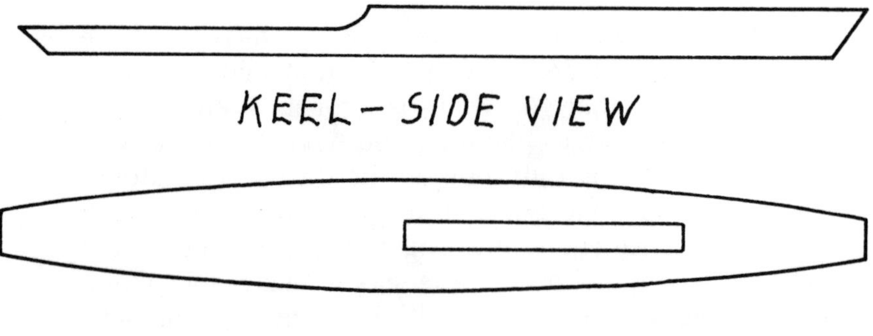

you more than a set of figures. Mr. Chapelle used to think that the size of the rudder and the *deadwood* aft—that's the underhang in front of the rudder and propeller—had something to do with it. But it's got nothing to do with it. It doesn't make any difference how much rudder you put on too short a centerboard or a centerboard too far forward. You're lost the minute you do it. It all has to do with locating the board at the center of lateral resistance. The shorter the boat on the waterline, the shorter the board can be. It's impossible to make a board that's too long, but of course that cuts into your cabin space.

All of this has to be in your mind when you cut the centerboard slot because you are doing it before the boat is ever built—unless you're like the people who recently built a big skipjack over at Solomons. They built their boat and then cut the slot, I'm told. I wouldn't want any part to that. Everybody to his own taste.

Cutting the slot goes rather quickly. You mark the center of the keel and then lay off parallel lines a half inch wider than the thickness of the centerboard. For a two-inch board you need a three-inch wide slot. When you have your lines drawn, you make a shallow cut into all of them with an electric saw. Then you take a two-inch auger—that's about as big as a man wants to handle-and bore holes half way through the keel about an inch apart. Then you roll the keel over and repeat the entire process. The auger holes won't meet exactly but it doesn't matter. The next step is to cut out the wood between the auger holes with a chain saw. This gives you a rough slot which all your shavings can fall through as you work it back to the electric sawlines with hand tools. You work with chisel and mallet and clean it up with a slice chisel, laying the keel on about a 45-degree angle so you will be comfortable working on it. Oak works nicely and so does pine, and if there's a nick or two up inside there it's of no consequence.

So far as shaping the rest of the keel, the only straight

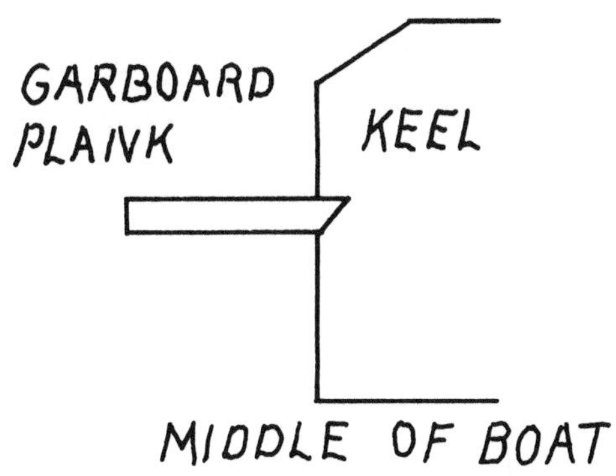

MIDDLE OF BOAT

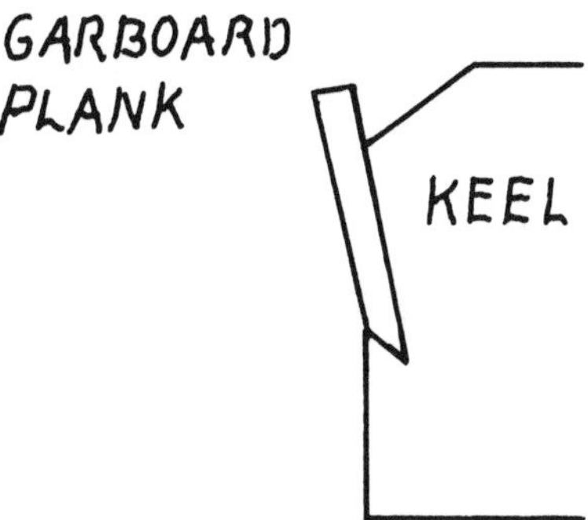

FORWARD END OF BOAT

Designers suggest putting a little hook in the rabbet instead of making it square. This way you won't force the garbord plank away from the keel when you caulk.

Centerwell logs might be 4 inches thick and a foot wide – The wider the better. You don't want anymore seams down in the water than you can help.

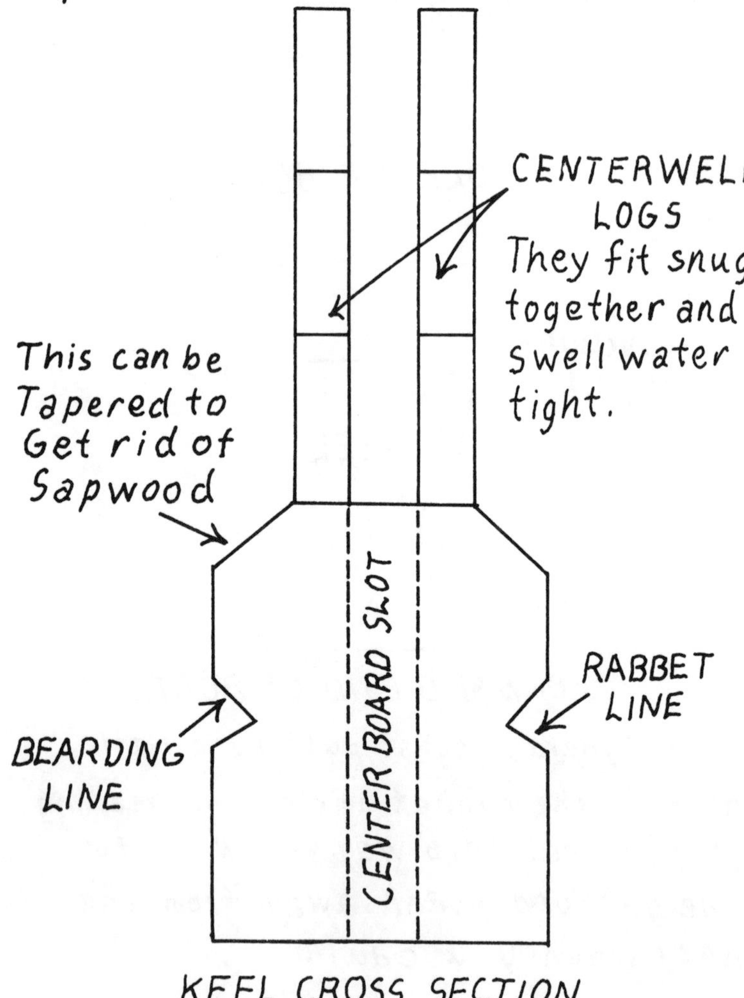

line will be along the bottom. Looking down from above, the keel will be drawn in forward of the centerboard slot and drawn in aft of it. Alongside the centerboard you want every bit of wood that the log will make: for strength, for holding fastenings, for holding the logs of the centerboard well and all that sort of business. You don't have to square off the top—it can be tapered to get rid of sapwood, as long as you leave four or five inches on each side to hold the well logs.

Looking at the keel from the side, it will be chopped down aft of the centerboard well so that the floors will lay across it. Forward of the well you let it stand proud the whole height of the log—you need all the wood you can get because it keeps getting thinner and thinner as you go forward. Generally by the time you get to the head ledge of the centerboard well you are to such a narrow part of the boat that the floor has to jump up anyhow, so you are not losing anything. The floors just have to be notched twice as much to fit over the keel.

The other thing you have to chisel out of the keel is the groove where the *garboard plank* will fit. That's the first plank going up. You have two lines for this groove. The *rabbet* line—the lower line—is something you put in right off because it is the outside line for the bottom of the hull. The upper line, called the *bearding line,* is almost impossible to put in accurately at this stage because it changes as you go forward and aft-it runs up higher and higher above the rabbet line the more your planking angles to the keel. In the middle of the boat you can hardly go wrong. Your planks are going to come out from the keel nearly at right angles. Fore and aft, however, it is best to cut a very shallow rough bearding line, making sure that you don't go up too high. To help make the line, you cut holes here and there and peg a batten along them to give yourself a marking edge. After all the frames are mounted you can just come along with the adze and finish chopping the bearding line in.

Stem & Sternpost

You have an inner stem and an outside stem. It's all one piece of wood except when you are building a skipjack. The inner stem is called the stem liner on the Bay and the stem apron when you go farther north. The planking fastens to it, as do the *knightheads,* the *knee* and the *breasthook.*

The outer stem is the *cutwater.* It takes the *bob chains* and the *longhead,* which is called the *gammon knee* outside the Chesapeake. There is nothing difficult about the stem and sternpost except that you have to be extremely careful when you bore a hole through the stem down at the cutwater to draw it back to the knee. You never put but one bolt in there—a big 3/4 inch bolt, and you have to take care not to get it into the part you will cut off when you shape the cutting edge of the bow.

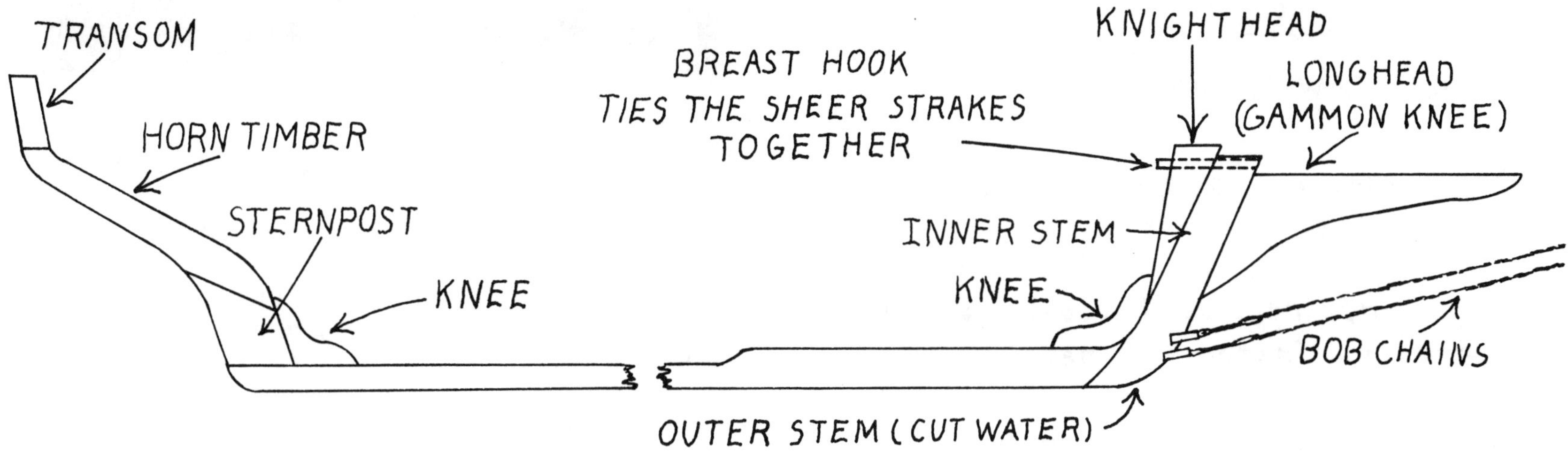

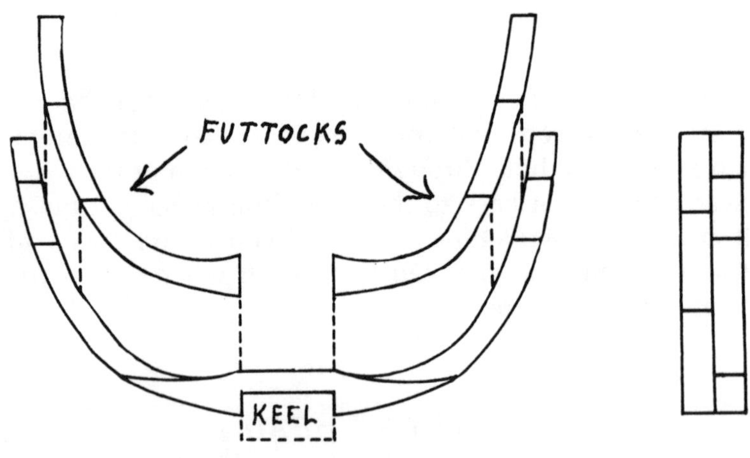

After they are cut the pieces are fastened together with bolts, hatch nails, spikes - something with a little girth. Our grandfathers used locust trunnels — tree nails — instead of metal.

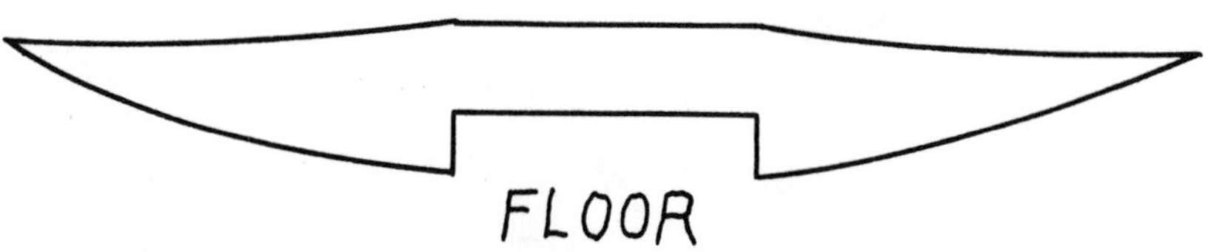

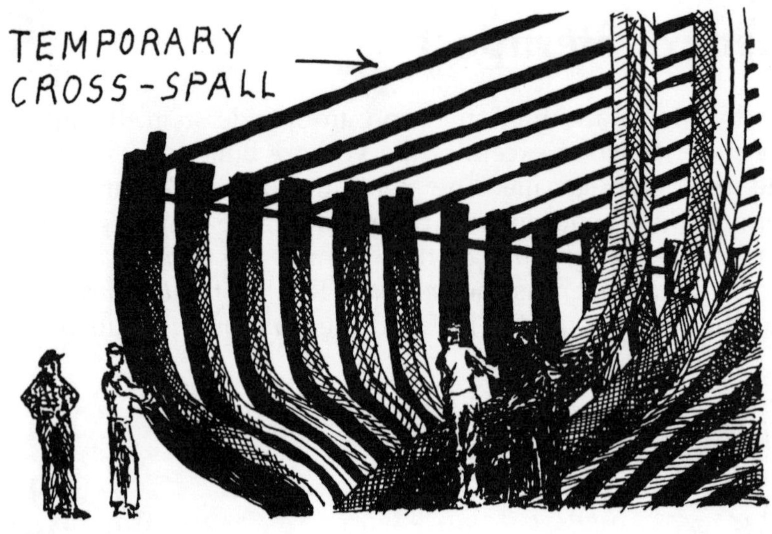

The Ribs—Working from a Model

The frames, or ribs, of a boat can either be steam bent from single long pieces of wood or sawn out of a number of pieces, doubled up and fastened together. For this book, we're assuming that they are going to be double-sawn, which is the regular old-time way, rather than steam bent, because for the kind of boat that people would normally build, it would take a whole lot more equipment, and a whole lot more knowhow, to set up a steamer, set up molds, and bend all these ribs on a jig.

In double-sawn frames, the bottom pieces, which fit over the keel, are called *floors,* and the parts that run up the sides are called *futtocks*—foot hooks. The frame pieces overlap more or less as shown in the drawing. For a 40-footer, the whole frame might be four inches thick doubled up. On this part of the Bay we build our boats a little heavier than they do on the Virginia side farther down the Bay. Even if it costs us more we think we come off with a better product.

Anybody who is building a boat and trying to make a dollar starts in the middle of her, when it comes to making the frames.

Here's how you do it, working from your wooden model. Usually you begin at home in the evening, on the dining room table. You put the model bottom side up, and use a couple of wooden wedges to make it exactly level in relation to the table. Then you take a piece of pasteboard—a milk carton, pizza box, anything that's nice and stiff. You draw a grid on the pasteboard, letting each half inch represent a foot, or however your model is scaled. You put one edge of the pasteboard on the table, and then you cut it and work it until the pasteboard fits exactly against the side of the model at the point where you want to make your frame.* Then you measure the edge you have cut out on the grid—so much in and so much up—for each half inch square. This gives you a *table of offsets,* which you write down on a piece of paper.

The next day, you go to the yard, where you have a big rough framing platform, as wide as the boat is wide and as deep as the boat is high, in other words as big as a crosssection of the boat would be at its widest point. This platform also has a grid pattern cut into it, actual size—one foot squares, made with an electric saw or a race knife so the lines won't erase.

The grid has the centerline of the boat marked on it and all of the grid lines are very precise. The platform is made of thick boards with gaps between them so that clamps can

be fitted. To make use of all this, we have a device, I don't know of any name for it, that consists of a flexible wooden batten, with long sticks attached to it. The sticks are made with nail holes so that they can be nailed to the platform to hold the batten in place. The device is designed so that a two-inch thick piece of frame can fit under it. I think you can begin to get the picture from this. You just take your table of offsets from the scale model and bend the batten around until it takes the exact same shape full size. Then you secure it with the nails. Then you begin shoving the framing pieces under it, marking them and sawing them to exact size one by one.

*There are probably ways to take the lines off the model with mechanical instruments, but the pasteboard method is simple enough. Some people get their measurements by making models that come apart in layers, or *lifts*, but these don't look so good later when you go to mount them on a wall plaque, as most builders do.

You start with the floor frame. To make this you need two measurements—the edge of it, which you get from the batten, and the slot in the middle where it fits over the keel. Of course you get that by going over to the keel and measuring it at the exact spot where the frame will go.

Next you make the futtocks, keeping them wide at the bottom and narrower as you get to the deck line—say 10 inches on the low part where they have to be notched to fit over the keel, 4 inches in the middle and 3 inches at the top. You run the top way past where you need it so you can fasten a temporary crosspiece, called a *cross-spall,* to hold everything in place while you are building.

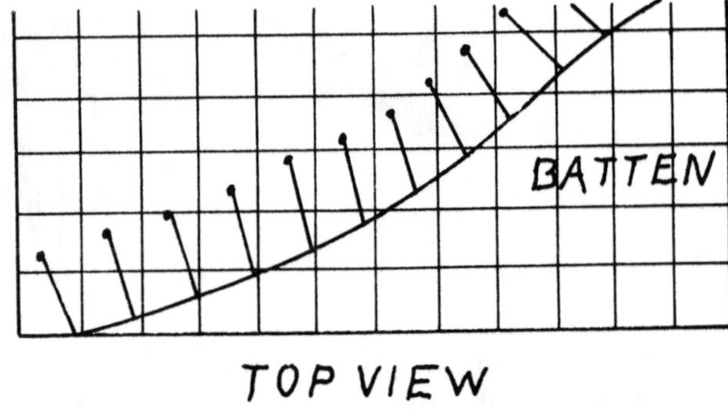

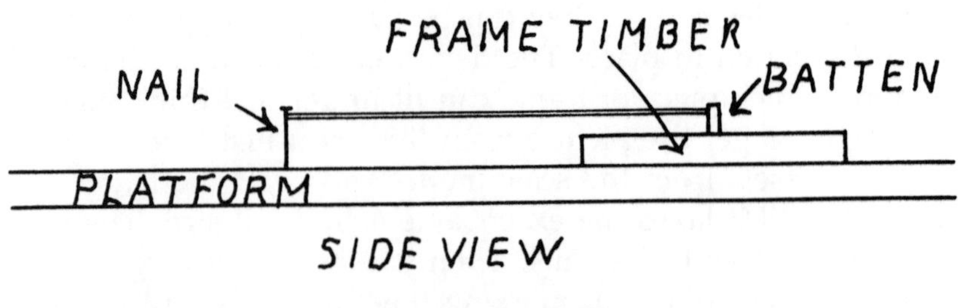

If you have followed all this, you will see that, so far, you only have made loose pieces half the thickness of the final frame. You lay these on the framing platform and use them to mark the other, overlapping pieces that will then be sawed out and fastened to them, making the frame perhaps 4 inches thick altogether on a 40-foot boat.

When you get one side of the frame finished you do the other side, using the same measurements. Then you have a big wishbone—a complete frame ready to go on the boat. There's really nothing to it. You can do it as fast as you can handle all that mess.*

Before you take a frame off the platform, you want to be sure you have marked the center line on the floor, using a race knife so you won't lose the mark. This is done on the forward side of the center frame forward, and on the afterside from the center frame aft. Also be sure to mark the deck line. And put a nail in the center of the temporary cross piece. This is for hanging a plumb bob in your next step.

Now you need to gather up all the people you know to help you set the frame on the boat. You level it with the plumb bob, and stabilize it by tying your crosspiece to the side of your building. If you are doing the boat out in the open you have to run something to a stake driven into the ground. It has to be stabilized.

On the *Norman,* where I was working by myself, I made the frames one side at a time—that was all I could lift. But I will really get some letters if I try to go into that method

---

*I would think that economics nowadays would make the system attractive even to people who build from blueprints. You could take your table of offsets and set up a platform and lay the grid on it and just get out your frames right there without going through all the effort of making molds—cut out the intermediate steps. The batten thing serves as your mold.

here. Builders here on the shore try to make a mystery of it. We say we hang the pieces from a clothesline.*

You don't need to go through the entire measuring procedure with every frame you make. For someone doing a 40-foot schooner, I would suggest starting with the three center frames. They are all exactly the same, and perfectly square on the edges. After you have these frames set up, then you would put another about three spaces aft, in each case using lines from your wooden model. I would call these pattern frames and the architects would call them stations. You would connect them with heavy battens, 2 inches by 2 inches, about 16 feet long and spaced about 18 inches to two feet apart. You would run the battens on just one side of the boat.

When the battens are set up we have another thing, I don't know if it has a name, that gives the shape for the intermediate frames by measuring from the inside of the boat. At the same time the battens show you the degree of angle for cutting the edges of the frames, so that the side planking will fit up flush and snug. This angle may change between top and bottom of the frame, so you have someone working the adjustment on the band saw as you cut it. If you miss on this you can work off the excess with an adze or electric plane. On the *Norman*, some of my frames shrank and I had to fill out with little shims, which is embarrassing to look at. Frames are never the showpiece of the boat. As you work the various pieces together on your platform you make them butt neatly but of course they will change shape by the time your friends come along to inspect your carpentry. Also you will want to use the full thickness of the lumber as it comes from the yard, so the pieces may vary a little in thickness.

The only difficult part of the framing is way up forward and way aft. Here you should have *cant* frames—they fit to the keel at an angle, so that the flat edge of the frame comes to the flat of the planking. You need about a half dozen forward and a half dozen aft. Architects show these frames running straight up and down on the blueprints, but that's because they draw them with a T-square. It looks pretty and nice, but if you build them this way you have a diamond-shaped frame that you can't get a fastening in. In order to draw a plank up to a frame you need to drive a nail square with it.

So you cant the frames, trying to hold the same spacing as the other frames about the middle of the way up. The floor part of the frame is made with a crooked piece to fit the cant. The farther forward you go the more crooked you need and the harder it is to find. But you can't avoid it unless you are drawing on paper with a T-square and making diamond-shape frames.

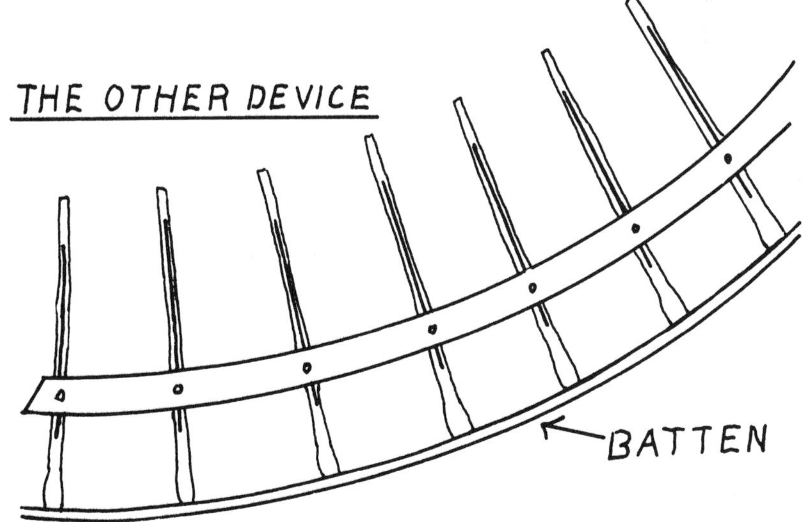

*Ed. note: In truth, the author used a method that even the most experienced boat builder would be loathe to attempt. After making the keel, he built the shelves—structural parts that determine the sheer or deckline. He suspended these from poles planted in the ground. This way he was able to insert the frames between keel and shelf, one side of the boat at a time.

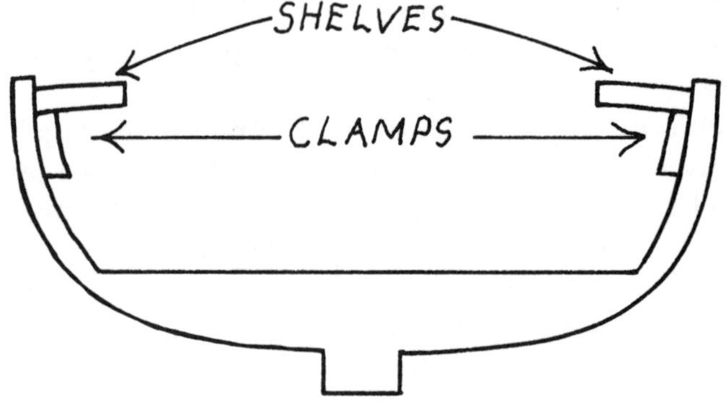

Once all of the frames are in, and stabilized to a degree, the next step is to put in long fore and aft pieces, one on each side of the boat, called *clamps*. The clamps are fastened against the inside of the frames, down from the sheerline by the thickness of the deck beams—four or five inches or whatever—so that the deck beams can rest on them. Along with the clamps, you will want to work in your *knightheads* at this point. These are large pieces at the bow that will help to receive the *hood ends* of your planking. I don't know why they call them hood ends. It just means the ends of your planks. The planks are always very narrow forward, so the knightheads give you a nice long space to get in three or four fastenings without destroying the ends of the planks with fastenings. In ships long ago, these pieces had heads of knights carved on them and they served as bits to hold dock lines—the lines were caught around what would be the neck of the knight. Nowadays they still have a hawse hole or chainpipe through them for docklines or anchor chain. To some people these holes are the "eyes" of the bugeye, though it's doubtful that this is how the bugeye got its name. Schooners and large skipjacks have them too.

On a boat of some size, say 60 feet or more, you would want to have a *shelf* on each side for additional strength. The shelf in a boat is like a plate on a house. It fastens edgewise to the frames and the deck beams land on it, instead of landing on the clamps. The clamps are lower, by the thickness of the shelves. The shelves fasten to the upper side of the clamps, the clamps fasten to the frames, and the frames fasten to the shelves, so you have a much stronger area than if the deck beams are just fastened down to the clamps. I have shelves on my bugeye, but that's because of the linty way I built it. Normally I don't think you would find them on a 48-footer.

The Sides

When the whole frame of the boat is completed, you turn immediately to the outside, and put in the sheer planking, or waist planking, or wale, or whatever you want to call it. This goes on as precisely as you can get it to the sheer of the boat. It consists of three parallel pieces bolted together on their edges and fastened to the edge of the frames the very best you possibly can since they are strength members. These sheer pieces would each be about four inches wide on a 40-foot boat and maybe two and a half inches thick—about three-quarters of an inch thicker than the rest of the planking. The bottom piece, the lowest of the three, has a *bead* in it which takes care of the transition from the thick part to the thinner lower planking.

After the sheer or waist is in, you will want to put a few deck beams across her to stabilize her, notching the ends of the beams a little bit here and there so that the top of the beam comes exactly even with the top of the sheer planking. Now you are ready for the rest of the planking. The individual pieces are, of course, called planks, but as you butt them together along the length of the boat, each line of planks is called a *strake*. You start laying them at the lowest point, the *garboard*, and work from the *garboard strake* out to the middle of the turn of the bilge. Then you go up underneath the sheer and begin to come down. Eventually you'll have a a gap of just one strake and you close that with your *shutter* strake which is the last strake of planking on the hull. Your shutter strake will be somewhere just above the turn of the bilge, which is the easiest place to put it in. Usually, at that point you call in your friends and have a little party.

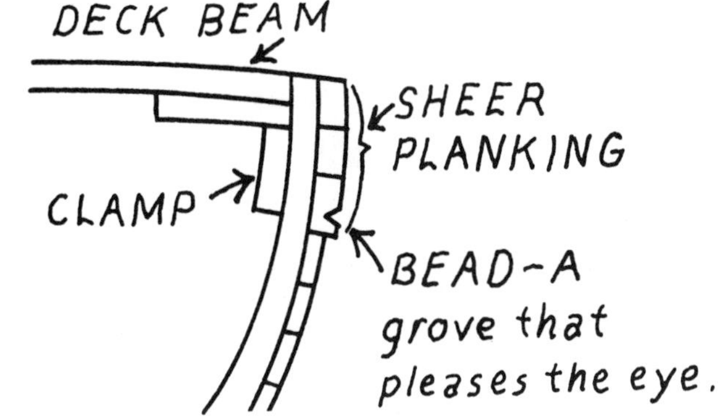

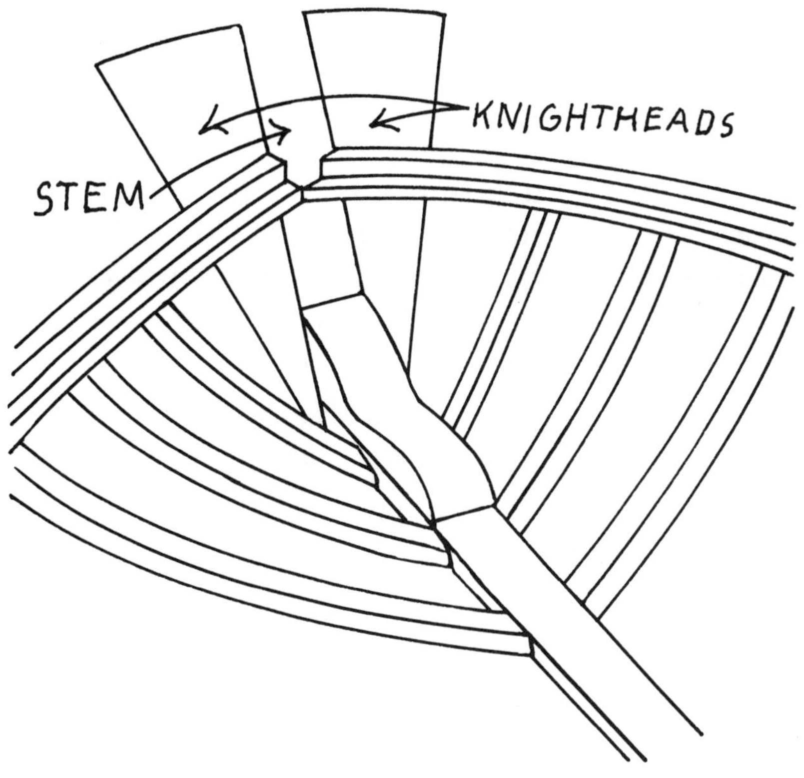

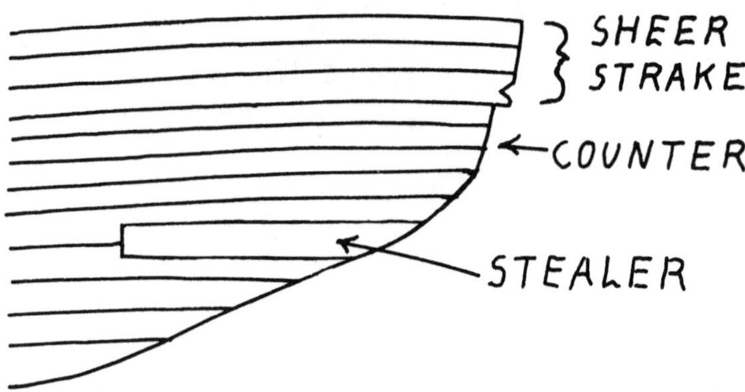

If you're building a schooner that's real deep aft, its just possible that you'll have to put in whats known as a stealer—a wedge-shaped plank that might run 12-16 feet in from the stern. These stealers make up the difference so that your strakes can come out right—Keep the same width—when they land on the counter.

It goes without saying that the frames must be prepped for receiving the planks. No frames can be set in a boat so exactly that there's no fairing necessary. Mostly you are off on your degrees more than you are on the shape of the frame. You will need to do a little planing, or heaven forbid, a little shimming here and there, to be sure the planks will fit right flat to the edges of the frames. You will also want to mark the frames here and there to help you get the measurements for the planks. Your strakes will be very narrow forward, and wider in the middle of the boat, but you want them to be the same width at each point—that is you want them to come out even, so that when it comes time to put in the shutter strake you don't have to put in a real narrow or a real wide piece. That would make the whole planking job look odd. Once you get past the first two or three garboard strakes, you will want, say, another 14 strakes up to the underside of the sheer planks, and you will want these strakes to persist forward, aft, and in the middle of her. To do this, first you mark your frames to show where each plank will come. I make little quarter inch sawmarks on the edges of the frames. Then as you come along with each plank you use what we call a spiling batten to get the measurement. This is a good batten with some camber or bend in it that holds its shape as you work with it. You lay it on your frames, guided by your little markings, and nail it here and there, wherever it comes. Then you take a set of dividers and mark a series of arcs on your batten, from the top of the last strake up on to the batten, or from the bottom of the last strake down, which ever way you are working. Then you take your batten over to the board you plan to use for the plank and mark the same arcs in reverse—marking from the batten on to the board. You connect your arcs with a line for sawing, making sure it looks good visually. This gives you one edge of the plank. You get the other edge by measuring at each frame, from the strake to your next sawmark. You mark these widths on your batten and connect them with a line, giving you the full outline of the plank.

You also take off and mark the degrees for the bottom edge of the plank. I usually write them down on a little piece of board or something like that. Every plank has a different degree at the edge of each frame. It doesn't change much from one frame to the next, but after you've gone four or five feet the difference is very noticeable, and if you don't get it right your plank won't fit the one below it.

With your spiling batten and dividers, there's no problem to get the shape of the plank. You just take it to the band saw and cut it. It always looks like a banana peel, you know. Unless it's very thick planking, you would normally work the degrees into the edge with a plane. You only worry with the lower edge. As you work up from the bottom you leave the top edge of each strake square, and then fit the next strake down to it, following the same procedure each time.

SPILING

The object is to transfer measurements from the boat to the board you want to cut.

STEP 1 Mark off width of planks on the frames, equal width on each frame.

STEP 2 Use dividers to transfer measurements to spiling batten.

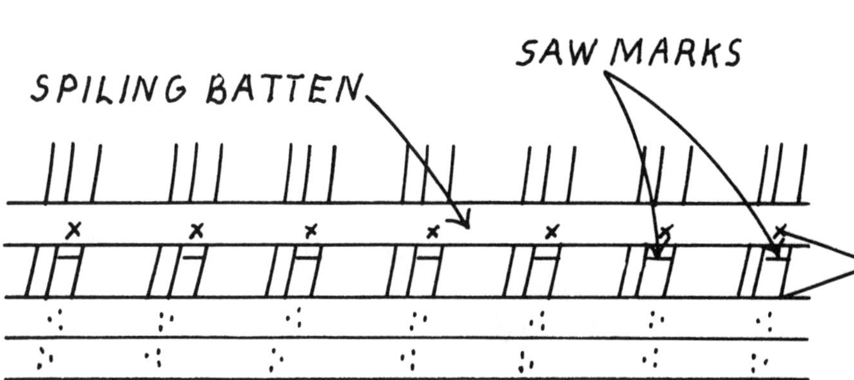

STEP 3 Use dividers, set up with the same arc, to transfer measurements from batten to board you want to cut. Get other dimension by measuring between previous plank and sawmark at each frame.

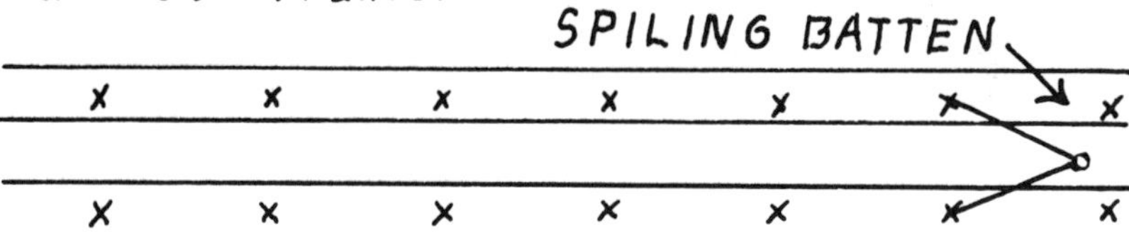

STEP 4 Connect Markings with visually fair line (no bumps). Saw out plank.

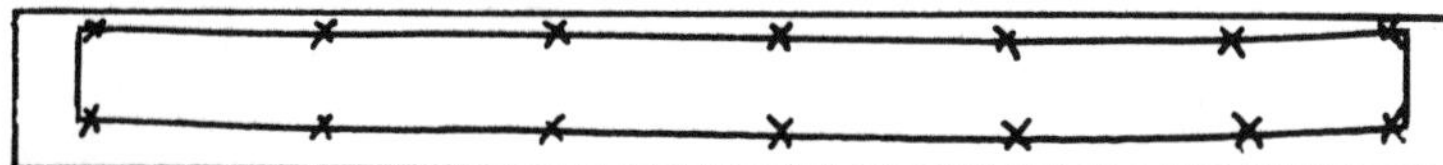

If your spiling batten wiggles up and down or edgewise or anything like that, then it's possible for you to get a plank that's either too much or not enough. You can try to "edge set" it, but that is rather a pain in the neck. On a ship they bore inch holes and put iron pins in them and then wedge between the pin and the edge of the plank to force the plank down. I've always been able to take a hydraulic jack or a chain clamp or something like that to pull them up or down. Sometimes you will happen to get a board with internal stress that will change shape after you saw it and then you will want to try to edge set it, rather than throw it away.

If you decide to steam, or boil, a plank, it will surely change shape because the hot water releases its internal stresses. But you can edge set a steamed plank without any trouble at all. Generally the first plank at either end of a strake-where the hull has its sharpest bends—will take care of what you have to boil or steam. After that the planking will take a natural bend.

When I was a young man, steam was used all the time—from the boiler that ran the mill. We had steam chests that would hold 40 to 50 pounds of pressure, enough to drive the live steam almost all the way through a three-inch plank. But when you take a steamed plank out of the chest you have a matter of moments to hang it completely before it sets. Then its over with.

If you boil the plank—saturate it with hot water—it will hold its heat lots longer. A man and his helper can handle a boiled board with all ease before it gets too hard to change it. I always boil a three-inch thick piece pretty near all day. One reason is you're always and forever short of help. Second is you just don't have to rush and fly about and all if the wood is thoroughly saturated. Even so, you've only got one hand to work with so you take all your clamps, malls, wedges and so forth and lay them up and down the line precisely where you will need them so you dont waste time. The quicker you get it on the better you are. If you have to boil one over again you're never as successful as you are the first time.

Author's Boiling Rig

Simple Rig

People say you can boil the thing two hours to each inch of thickness, which gives you four hours of boiling for a two-inch piece. I think if the oak is half seasoned, and is a good grade, you can give it a good rolling boil for three or four hours and that will be enough. You'll be able to bend it.

I do mine in a 16-inch piece of dredge tube that's joined to a double boiler. You build a fire on the side of the thing. The water is jacketed all the way around the fire box so that I can boil water in 20 minutes from cold.

If I was only going to build one boat I'd never go to the work I did with this boiler. I'd just take a big pipe—like a culvert in a road, a portion of a smokestack, any long tube—and stop one end of it, caulk it up and build a fire under it. You would cock up the other end about 20 degrees. You lose an awful lot of heat but it is a workable device. You always stick the small end of your plank in first because the small end is always the end that's bending the most. Also you have to watch to be sure you don't boil your water away and scorch the plank before you realize the water is gone. This almost always destroys the plank.

To protect the planks, it's best to alternate the nail holes as you work down the frames—two and one, one and two, two and one, as shown. The wider the plank the better, so far as getting spikes into it. If you have an 8 or 9 inch plank there's no problem getting three or four spikes in it. If you put a lot of spikes in a piece that's only four inches wide you cut it in two with your fastenings. Even with a six-inch plank, when you bore three 3/4-inch holes for the heads of the spikes and the plugs, you are taking out about a third of the surface. So a wider plank is better if your turns are easy and you can get it around your bilge. Our fathers had the theory that the wider the plank, the stronger she was on her sides. You know a board 12 inches wide is stronger edge-wise than a 6-inch board.

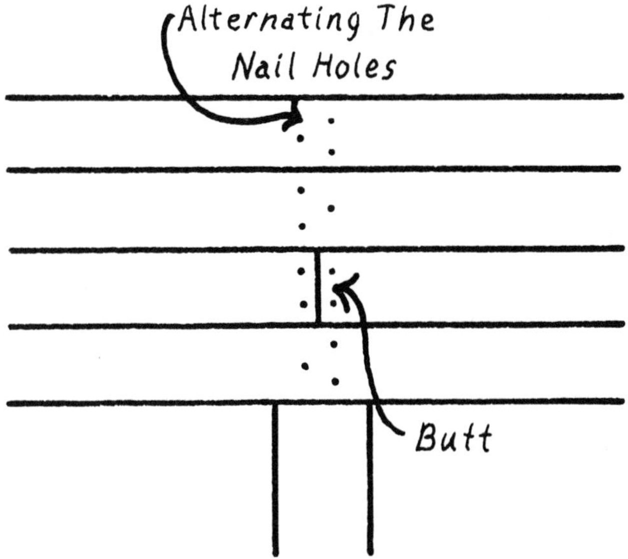

Planks generally butt at the frames. The idea of separate butt blocks is Johnny-come-lately; our fathers never fooled with them. Nail holes are alternated from plank to plank.

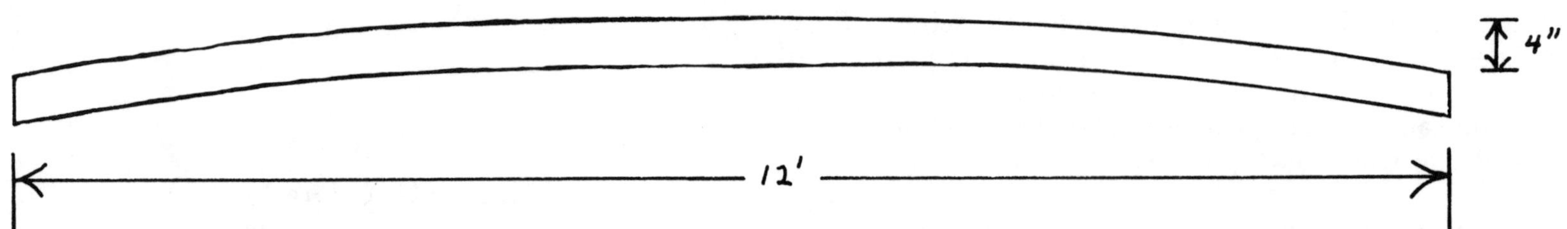

Deck beams follow a perfect arc, with 4 inches of rise for every 12 feet of length.

To make your pattern beam — the model for all of your beams — you send someone out with a steel tape to a point on the ground 60 feet from you. This gives you exactly the right radius for drawing the arc on your pattern beam.

The Deck

Once the boat is planked for sure, if you're going to *ceil* her—cover the inside of the frames—now is the time to do this. You can stand up and work inside her without too many deck beams getting in your way. If you are not going to ceil, then you are ready for your deck framing. Our work boats, the dredge boats on the Bay, have a rather flat deck, because the deck is actually a working platform. We follow the practice of the old time builders-four inches of camber to every 12 feet of deck beam. It doesn't matter if the beam is 16 feet long or 20 feet or four feet, it's still a 4-inch rise to 12 feet in a perfect arc so that you can lay your pattern on the rough material and not have to center it. You don't have to center the beams on the boat either. If you have one a little long it can be sawed off at either end or both ends and still have the same camber going across, as long as it's cut with a perfect arc.

Generally what decides the spacing of your deck beams is the size of your *cargo hold* or *deck house*. You put an extra strong beam forward and aft of the hold or house. So after you decide where the holds are going and where these extra heavy beams are going to be put in, you space the rest of your beams accordingly. You have to remember that you have two masts to consider and a snubbing bit or *samson post*. You can't have these running through the middle of a deck beam. So you keep these features in mind that are going to come up later and try to space your beams so that you can get the samson post just aft of the forward deck beam and the masts in between the beams. If you have *lodging knees* they'll go between the deck beams that the mast steps between. I've never seen these put where the snubbing bit is on a Bay boat, but if you're going to build a little ship or period vessel they go everywhere, all up and down her.

SNUBBING BIT — called Samson Post because of its strenghth.

Locust is a good wood for the Samson Post. It's strong and won't rot.

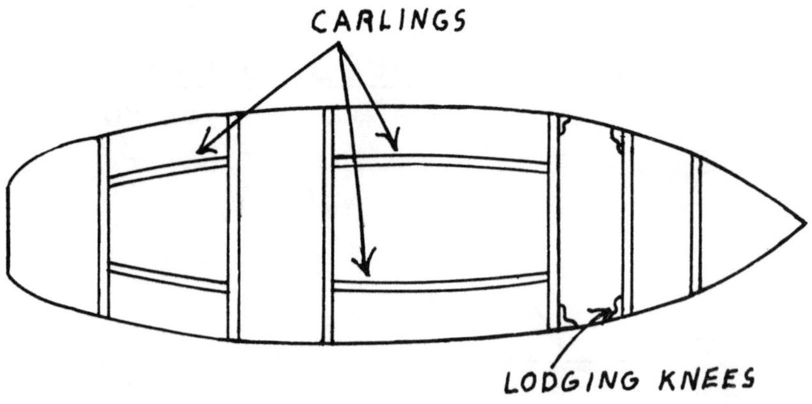

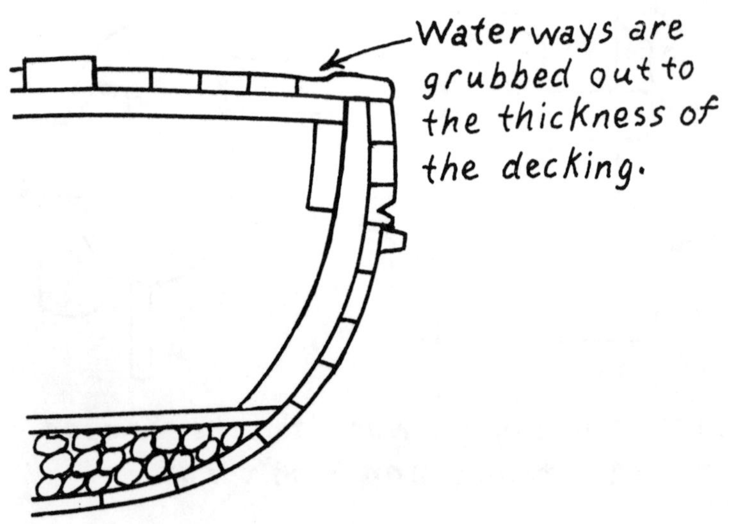

After you place your deck beams, you put in the fore and aft pieces, which are called *carlings.* You especially need these to support the short beams that run from the side of the deck over to the hatch holds, or deck house. After the carlings are in, then come the *covering boards,* or *waterways,* at the outer edge of the deck. These are long, very thick pieces, made of the very best material you can find. The old timers were always made of Georgia pine. Since then we've had a lot of trouble finding the right material. I've seen them oak. I made mine of cedar because I had it. I had pine cut for them but when I got hold of cedar I used it because it was so much better, so far as resisting rot and prolonging the life of the boat. It is such a vulnerable area.

The outer edge of the waterways is fastened to the sheer strakes and the inside edge is fastened to the deck beams. The ends of the frames come up under them. I generally cut my frames short a little bit so the air can get between the covering board and the head of the frame. I pour hot paraffin on the heads of all of them, to seal them from any moisture that might get there. I don't know if that makes any sense. It might make more sense to let them come up to the covering boards and give them a coat of some fungicide and fasten the covering boards right into them.

You begin your decking with the centerplank, or kingplank, which you carry all the way down the center of the boat. It goes out between the knightheads forward, covers the inner stem and goes out as far as the outer stem where the tenon is that holds the underside of the bowsprit. The samson post goes through it, and it runs on aft where it helps to form the *mast partners*—the mast steps through it. Of course if you are going to have a two-master, you have a king plank that pretty well runs the length of the boat, interrupted only by the hatches. I used a 20-inch wide oak plank at the after end of the *Jenny Norman* because it's going to receive all the thrust of the steering gear.

When I was putting in the kingplank I discovered that the boat was an inch and a half wider on one side than the other. I doublechecked her as I was going along, pulling a line through her and dropping a string down and trying to hold the center, but some time or other there got to be a difference there. I don't know when it occurred. I've looked at her side and I can't see any bulge in it. I just don't know. When I put in the kingplank I found that the center was about 3/4 inch to one side for a distance of 15 or 20 feet. I didn't want to put everything 3/4 inch over, so I put the kingplank and masts down the middle of her sighting from stem to stern, and that let her be twice 3/4 wider on one side in that one area. I put the waterline on her from the deck down instead of putting it from the ground up. That way if she floated a little higher on one side than on the other I could correct it with ballast.

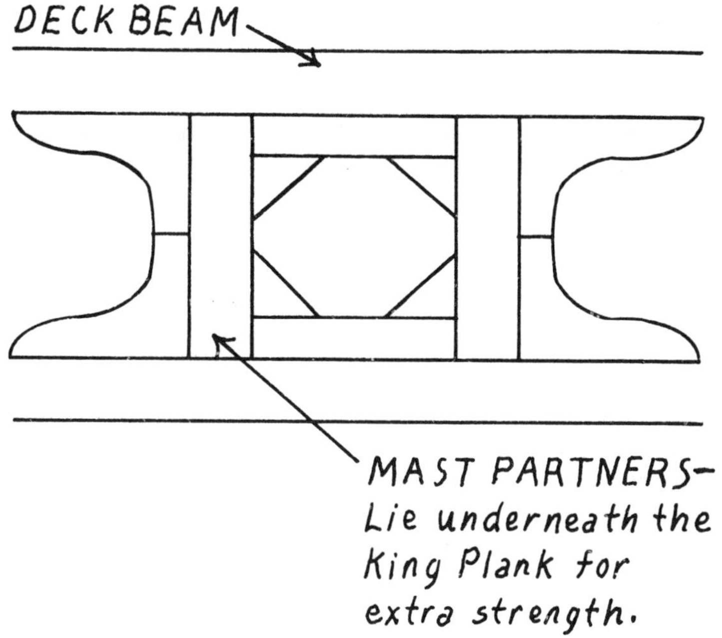

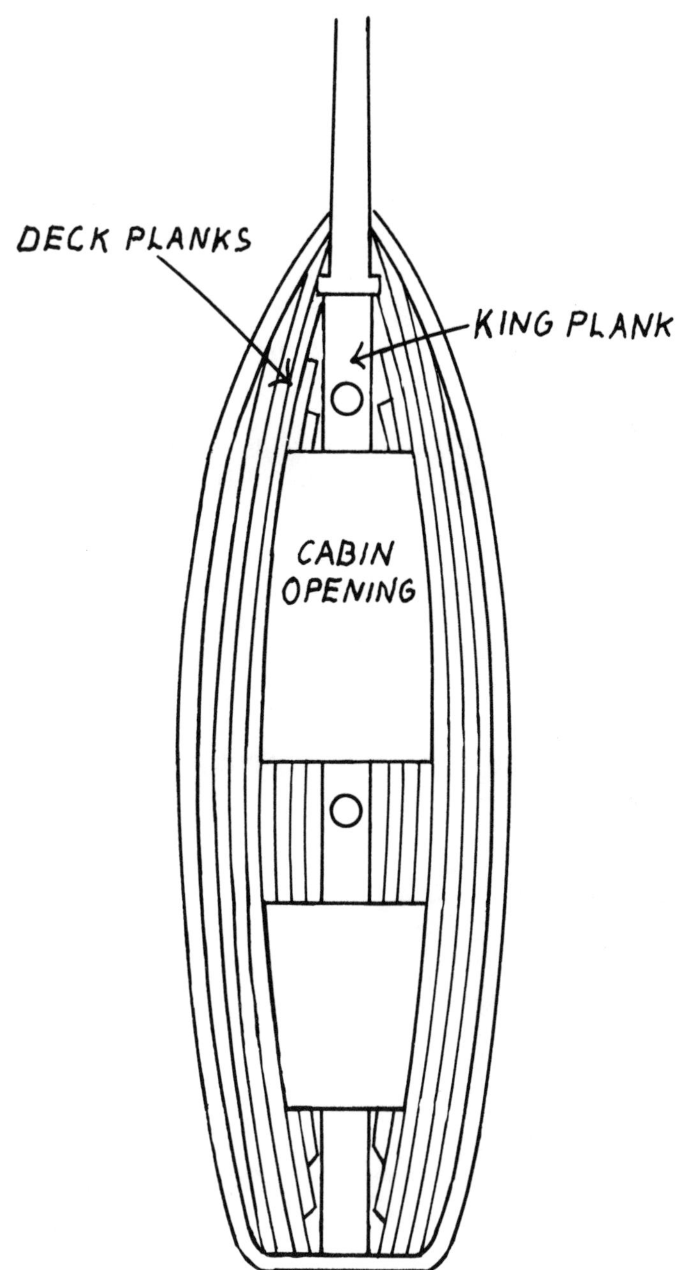

Great care should be taken with the deck because it has to do with the life of the boat—how long it will last. If you've got a leaky deck you soon lose your boat. All the beams, all the carlings, everything rots right out of her if the deck leaks.

The decking should be edge-grained of the best materials you can get your hands on. A lot of the little sloops that were built down here around Madison were decked with 2 x 2 white pine, edge-grained. I used yellow pine, two inches thick by two and a quarter wide. I wish it was all edge-grained but it's very difficult to get that much material edge-grained any more

I started my deck around the sills of the house, which exactly follow the lines of the sides of the boat. I carried the lines all the way along, springing the planks in on the forward quarter where it starts to become very narrow. Of course you can't bend it that much at the bow and it would be foolish to do that anyway. You would get long feather edges on your planks where they come alongside the kingplank, which is not practical or watertight. You can't fasten or caulk a long feather edge. So I put margin pieces up forward coming down along the kingplank and butting into the other planking. You need a butt to caulk.

I caulked my deck with oakum twine. I outgauged the deck—opened up the seams of the deck—to receive the oakum and we got along just fine with it. I was able to buy oakum that was well saturated with tar and it saved me from using the mess of jute that we're getting now in place of oakum. It's nearly impossible to find oakum any more. Oakum was hemp, same as hashish, and those people that make those laws haven't got brains enough to know that you can't smoke hemp after it's been tarred. They just cut off all hemp.

I drove the oakum down 3/8 inch and then poured pitch on top to fill the seam. Pitch is from pine tar. It's a derivitive of the turpentine industry, and very hard to come by. We found three tubs of it in Georgia when we built the *Dove*. It's hard pine resin—exactly what you put on a violin bow—so you have to heat it 'till it smokes. Come the first hot summer, your pitch will soften and work itself down some into the caulking and you will need to repitch it then, filling the seam while the weather is hot, but that should be the last time it will be pitched for 10-15 years. The hotter the weather gets and the more the decks shrink, the deeper this stuff settles in, sealing all the time. That's unlike these rubber sealants they have nowadays. The rubber has this tremendous press—like Cuprinol, and everybody thinks that's great stuff—but it shrinks under the ultraviolet rays of the sun. You can use it after cotton, but you can't use it after oakum because oakum puts oil on the sides of the seams, and the rubber sealant is absolutely no good where there's oily wood or any oil on the deck. I've already given my decks two coats of boiled linseed oil and will continue to oil them because it's compatible with the pitch and the tar. I'll oil them as long as I can. When I see that the oil is beginning to give way or the decks are beginning to take water I'll paint them, but I might let them go a good long while, as long as they'll take oil.

Dry rot is the bane of a wooden boat. It is caused by a fungus that thrives in damp places, especially places that are wet and dry, wet and dry, from rainwater leaking in. The preventive course for rot is good lumber (no sapwood), well-bedded seams, insides of hull periodically saturated with oil and fungicides, and an annual coat of paint. I've seen them with manufacturer's plaques saying the boat was treated with this or that famous preservative, and the inside was a mess. They hadn't kept after it over the years.

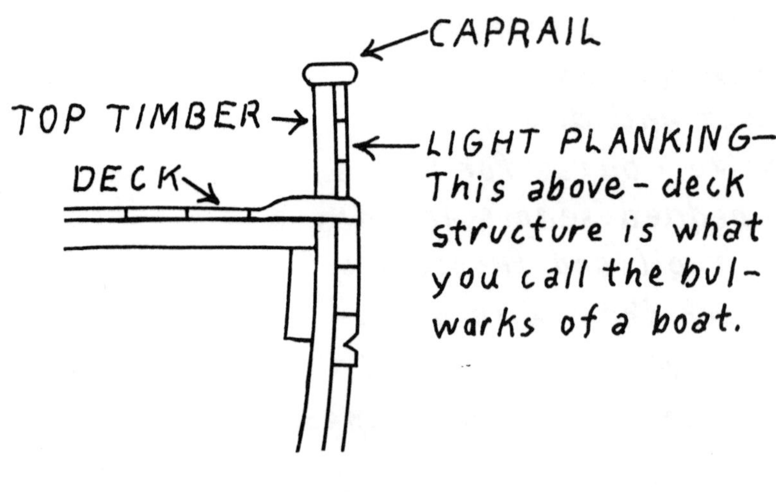

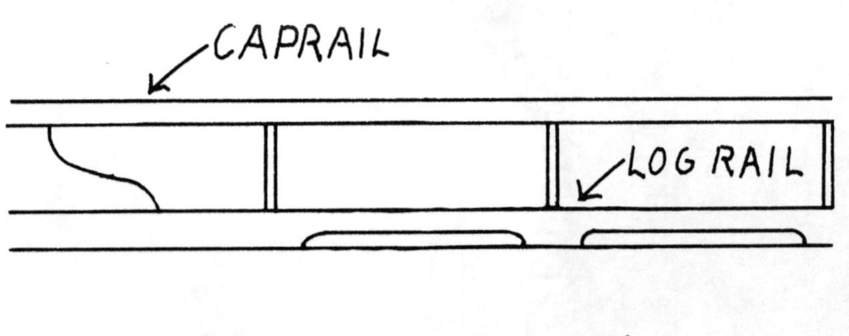

Top Timbers and Caprails

If you are building a schooner, after your decks are on, you need to cut your openings in the waterways for the top timbers. Any hole you cut in the topside of a boat is something to think about, because it exposes you to possible rot, so it must be done with precision. The top timbers are shoved down through your openings, fastened to the waist plank and wedged with cedar shingle wedges. Then the opening is sealed with caulking and pitch or something of the sort. Then you begin to put your caprails on. These are strength members so they are always heavy—three inches thick, eight or ten inches wide.

They are housed out underneath and set down on top of the timbers to stabilize them. One drift bolt is driven down into the end of each timber, with a forelock—I think they call them clinchermans nowadays—and that's all that holds the cap down. A little thin planking—like three-fourths of an inch-goes underneath the caprail down to within an inch of the waterways, leaving enough space so that any water you take aboard can be gotten off quickly.

I've seldom seen top timbers and caprails made of anything but oak, except on a yacht where the rails might be mahogany. One time I put on a set of caprails that were teak, but I never expect to put on another at the price of teak now.

On a bugeye you do not have top timbers. You run a log rail all the way along the edge of the washboards and put the caprail above it on little short stanchions. Nowadays these are made of plastic so they won't rust.

Bits

The stern *bits* on the *Norman* are mounted into blocks set into the deck. They are fastened down extra good inside, so the wake from the outboards won't pull them up while she's riding at the dock. I don't fasten them to the deck directly because I've seen them pull the deck right up, after a time.

You know about sailboaters and outboarders. My wife and this friend of hers were talking on the porch one day. She told my wife that they had just gotten themselves a new boat. It finally came out that they had bought an outboard. My wife said we had never had one—we were almost dedicated sailboat people. The friend said, oh, we don't like sailboat people. They're so unpleasant. Well, my wife was shocked. She said she never heard that about sailboat people. The friend said, oh yes, when you run by them, they're always dashing here and there and looking over their shoulder and giving you the hardest looks and don't speak or anything like that. Come to find out, he'd taken his new outboard and gone over to Haines Point in Washington and was water-skiing her through a moth race—turning her through all those little teeny sailboats. My wife allowed that, no, they don't appreciate motor boats running through their races.

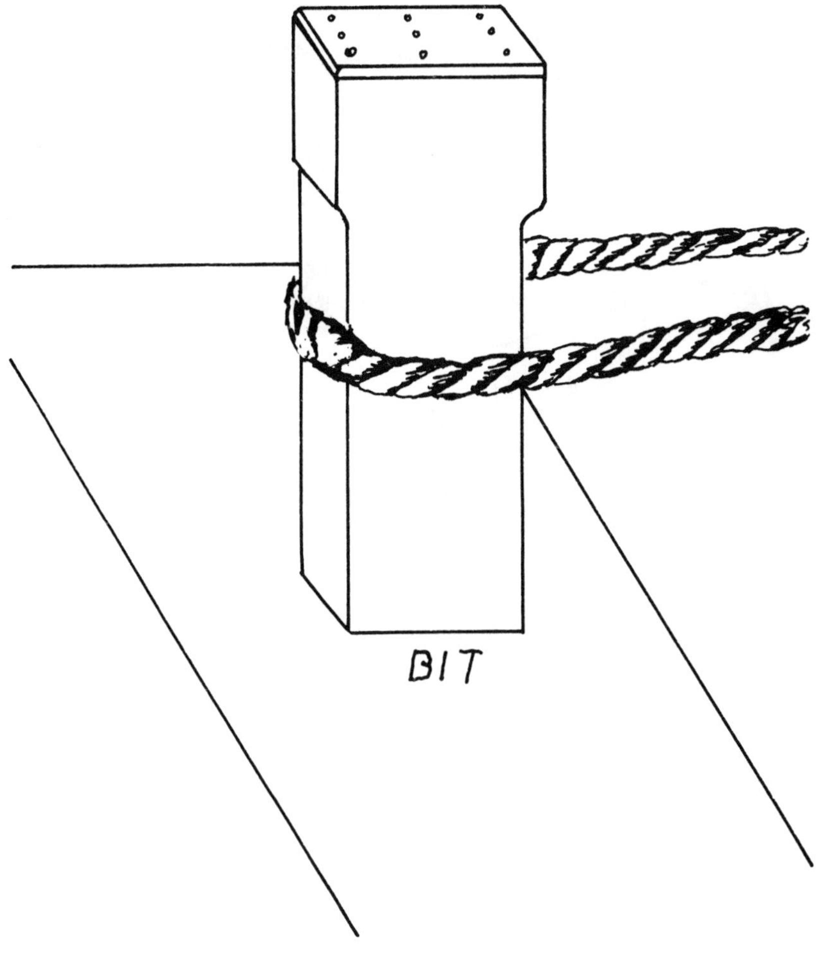

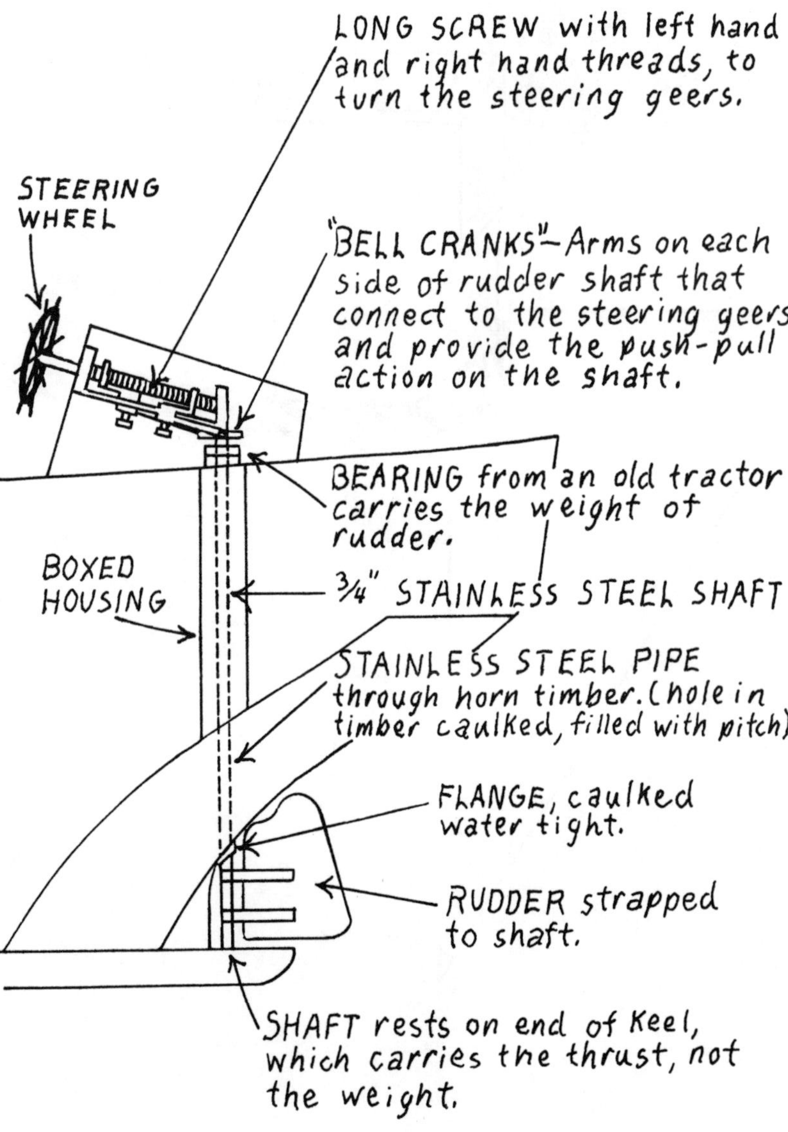

The Rudder

I've never seen anyone try to tell you what size of rudder you should have. If you dish out beans on your plate to eat, you know how many beans to dish out. No one is going to say that's too many or that's not enough. Mr. Chapelle's rudders were all too big, but that's much better than to have them all too small. The only time a small rudder will do is on a powerboat, where the thrust of the propwash turns the boat. With a boat under sail, it is important to have a rudder that reaches down to good hard water, beneath the turbulent surface water. The early boats had deep, small rudders, but they weren't that maneuverable. The rudders were all handled by hand, and as they got bigger they became more difficult to handle. It took several men, and if they were working it in a following sea it just about killed them. The strain was eased by gearing, by use of wheels to steer with instead of steering directly with a big tiller, and in some cases by putting a three or four inch leading edge on the rudder so it catches some water on the opposite side of the boat, helping you to turn it and hold it over.

There are several ways of attaching the rudder, depending on the boat. Skipjacks generally have hinged or "barndoor" rudders, while schooners and most of the bugeyes have "plug" rudders where the rudder post is housed in the deadwood, to reduce turbulence. But you can't put a leading edge on this kind of plug rudder.

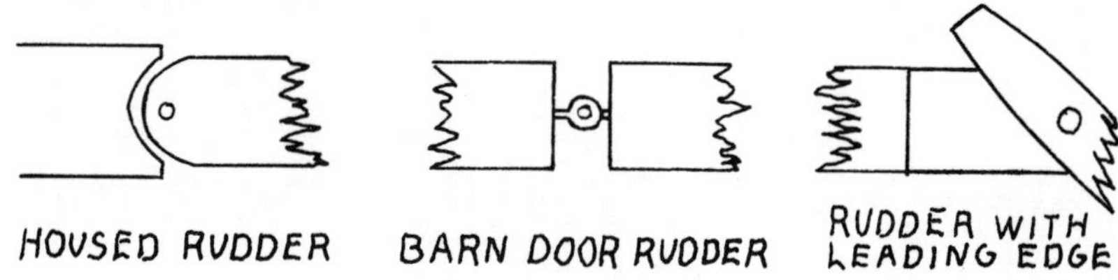

The Bowsprit

On the Bay we have a general rule for the bowsprit: it is as long, outboard, as the width of the boat on deck. All the shape is put in the top and sides. Inboard, the bowsprit follows the sheer of the deck, but as you reach the outer end it matches the horizon. The stay at the outer end—the jib or head stay—must be kept tight in order for the boat to sail close to the wind, and the easiest way to keep this stay tight is to tighten the turnbuckle on the bob chains down at the stem of the boat. As you do this over a period of years the end of the bow sprit begins to look hogged down a little. The purpose of the bowsprit of course is to help you carry sail. On a schooner you have a flying jib boom extending out beyond the bowsprit and this lets you carry as many as four headsails—a staysail, jib, flying jib and jib topsail. We'll get into this later on. If the boat is light-headed—out of balance—you can change the outer sails without too much expense, compared to the staysail which lands on the bowsprit.

The chopping of the bowsprit goes very quickly. At the inboard end you cut a tenon which goes into the samson post. On the underside you make a good size slot—say 2 1/2 inches wide, 3 inches deep, 8 to 10 inches long—for a tenon that you form at the top of the stem of the boat. These two tenons hold the bowsprit in place while the knightheads cradle it and keep it from rolling.

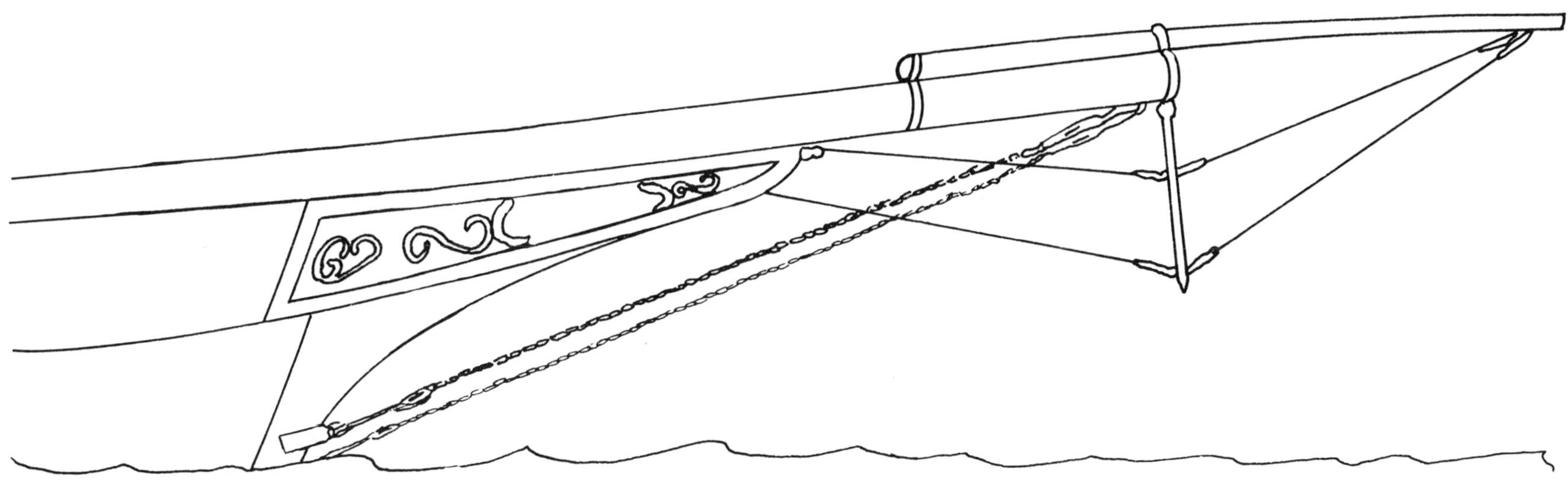

Chapter 5

Arranging the Living Space

You're ready now for the inside of her. The plan is most important. You have to know how many people you want to accomodate, and whether you want them to go in luxury or whether you want them to go spartan or half and half. You have to know how many ladies will be included on most of the trips that she takes because you have to have a different setup for ladies than you do for a bunch of men who are just going to drink beer. As soon as ever this is all arranged and agreed upon then you begin to lay out the quarters and accomodations.

The considerations are the location of the galley, the location of the head, the berths—you have to arrange for them so that they are as easy as possible to take care of when it comes to making beds. If you can only get to one side of a berth it's harder to make it up than it is if you can get down one side and across an end. When you have berths coming down the side of a cabin it's a good thing to have a hanging locker or some kind of cabinet between the ends of them so that there'll be a little bit more privacy than if you just put a board up between them.

You have to think about water. Are you going to have hot water? Are you going to have a shower, and the machinery that goes with it? There's right much to be considered when it comes time to trim one out and actually I have never done one myself that was ideal when it was finished. Almost without fail you can never get one that will suit a majority of the ladies. There'll be more against than there will be for it by a large percentage. The girls that have lived aboard boats for an extended period are the easiest ones to do for. I'm sure the reason is that they've had first hand knowledge of the thing and they've long since realized that you can't have all the comforts of home aboard a small boat.

The layout of the *Norman* provides for two separate cabins. From fore to aft, the first thing you have is a rope or chain locker. That's a slatted affair, well ventilated. Immediately after that are two double berths, back and shoulder sized on the after ends but narrower forward—pie shaped. At the ends of the berths are some chest-high lockers. This forward part will be the most private of her quarters, other than the after cabin. Next come the transom berths, single berths with two down each side with cupboards between them. One set is directly opposite the table which hinges off the centerboard trunk and is long enough to seat four, and in a pinch, six people. After the table comes the galley, on one side of the trunk, and head and shower, on the other side. Both are directly accessible from outside through the hatchway, although they aren't all that accessible to each other because of the trunk running beween them. You can't have everything.

Behind the main cabin is a little cargo hold for all the boat's stuff—anchors, scuba gear if you have that, extra life preservers, extra of everything. Her fuel tanks are in there, her battery box is in there, everything that makes such a mess out in the boat is in there. It's like her attic that you clean out every five years. The hold has two hatches for ventilation, just big enough for a person to slip through and hand things up. There's a small iron ladder on one side.

The after cabin is a combination of cabin and engine room, but more cabin than engine. The engine is under a demountable box, the lid of which serves as work table for charts or whatever. It is located immediately at the bottom of the companionway ladder so it has easy access. Two berths are down there, along the sides. It is kind of the captain's private room. From it you also have access to the *lazarette,* which is in the very back, under the fantail. That's where you put the canned tomatoes. There's right much space in there, as much space as the smaller boats have altogether, square feet-wise.

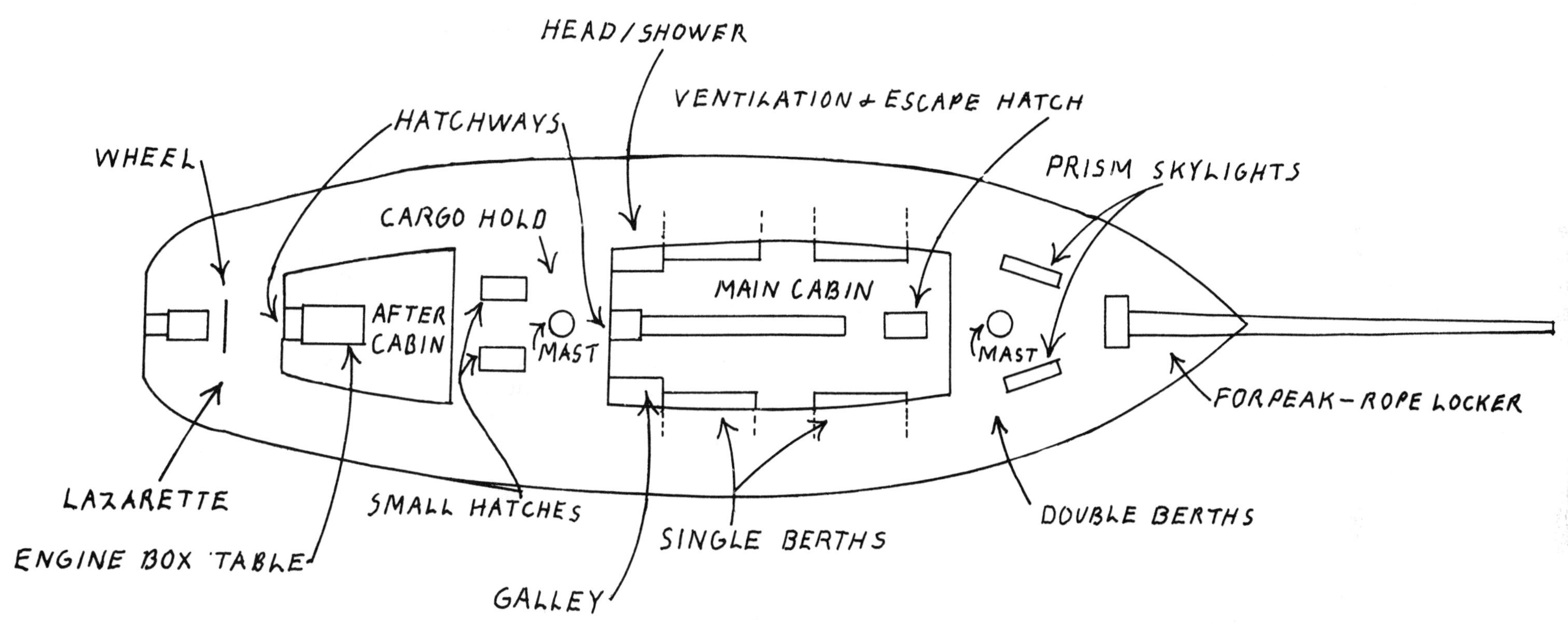

JENNY NORMAN INTERIOR LAYOUT

The Deck House

In building your deck house, you have to ask yourself, where is the boat going to be used? Is she going outside, in blue water? If so, you've got to think about a cabin that's as strong as any other part of the boat, or it'll wash off of her. The cabins of our old schooners were four inches thick. The corners were dovetailed, and the sides and ends had rods that went all the way through the deck, and were nutted underneath, so that they couldn't explode—come apart—and they had no framing in them.

I did my bugeye the same way. The only framing on my cabin is near the middle, to help carry the sides where the portholes have been cut and where I have some knees to carry the roof. Other than that the cabin is not framed up as such. There are no corner posts on the main cabin. They're so vulnerable. If the least bit of water gets around there it rots the whole business out. If I don't have any of that I can see what's going on.

The sides and ends of my cabin come down and rest on the sills. Inside I have a ledge facing off the carling and the sill and finishing off all that stuff. The little framing that I have comes down to that ledge. The roof beams lay on a shelf that runs the full length of the insides of the house and stand out about four inches. Several of the beams are dovetailed to the sides fo extra strength. I was able to get a good substantial roof on it that was 1 3/4 inches thick, caulked with oakum and paid up with pitch.

You never run the ends of the deck house up from the deck with a square. You have to compensate for the sheer of the deck. A ninety degree angle would pitch the ends forward or back, depending on which end of the boat you are on. It would look like the devil. Likewise, you don't run the roof on the house in a straight line between the two ends. That would make it look humped. The eye concentrates on the deckline, and the roofline should follow that. The sides of the house should pitch in a little, about half a bubble on your level, so they don't look fat.

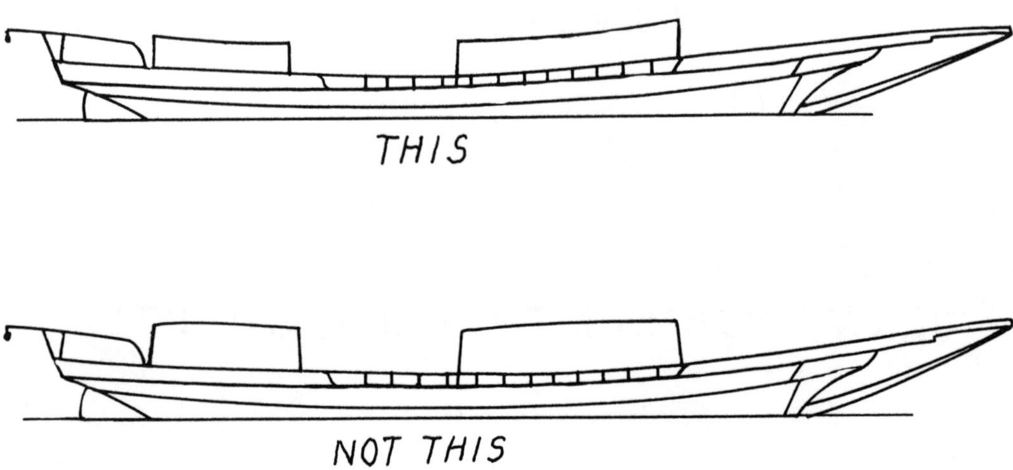

An engine can be moved out of the cabin without tearing up the deckhouse. You take a utility pole and balance it on the boom of a crane. You shove the pole in the companionway over the top of the engine, chain the engine to the pole, bear down on the out end of the pole, swing back on the boom and bring the engine out of the hole. It's simple, but there'd be plenty of yachtsmen who would tear the house lid off. On the Norman, if worse came to worse, the whole house could come off, using four hydraulic jacks underneath the corner posts. Some of the drift bolts would come up with the house, some would stay in the sill. You'd have to fasten it back some other way.

I suppose it will surprise everyone, but I use plastic portlights in the deckhouse, instead of bronze. They don't run green down the side of the boat. More important than that, they have sills set on an angle so that they dump the water out when you open them. The bronze ones drop the water on you every time. The plastic are lighter, easier to install, and best of all, come at half the price. You can get them from the Fuller Brush Co. They have a little marine division that's run by one girl. You call there and she'll tell you what she has and how much it costs and the whole business.

The hatch slide is very important on a yacht because there are so many of those things that leak. I suppose there are as many ideas of how one should be made as there are people who make them, but they all come back to one basic design—the pull-over cover that slides on runners. On small boats they have to run fore and aft—there's not room to run them crosswise—so you have to be sure the water can't rush under the foreward end when the cover is closed. During World War II the government people designed a bonnet that protected the foreward end. The hatch slid under it. It was surely a help, but it was a lot of work to build it, and there was never any way to get underneath of it for maintenance. You shut yourself out from ever taking care of anything under that bonnet. The government could care less. Their designers are not aware of the importance of keeping everything so you can get your hands on it and maintain it.

Anyway, you can make a hatch that is watertight and satisfactory but it's not a job that you can fly out there and do in a few hours. You need to take care and time.

On the *Norman* I have a forward hatch that you can go out of quickly if anything happens at the galley. Some locust pins serve as a ladder down below. The normal purpose of this hatch is light and ventilation. I have a hinged skylight over it. Normally they are made longer than they are wide, which makes a pretty skylight. But to heck with pretty this time. Mine is perfectly square so it will fit over the hatch however you set it on. I can hinge it up fore and aft the normal way, or I can turn it and scoop in the air from ahead. Or, if I'm driving through a sea, I can just open the rear to draw air out without letting anything in.

I've got four strong half-inch rings on the deck, two on each side, to hold that thing down in a sea, so you don't have to depend on toggles inside of it to hold it. You just take nylon rope and go over the top of the thing and through these rings and lash it down.

You can just imagine if that thing washed away from you. Mr. Chapelle was called by the insurance company one time to inspect one of the first large fiberglass boats, 50 feet or so, an auxiliary sailboat with a nice diesel in it. She was coming up from St. Thomas with the owner and his wife and their two sons and their wives—six people altogether. The sons and their wives had left their children home and were coming with the old folks to bring the boat home. They were almost to Bermuda when they ran into heavy weather. The Coast Guard began to get their Maydays. The weather was so heavy and the going out there so slow that by the time the Coast Guard got to the last location it was dark and they could see absolutely nothing.

The wind abated and in a day or so someone happened along and reported a big oil slick running down the Gulf Stream as far as they went. The Coast Guard went out and found where it had sunk. The insurance company was excited-they'd lost six heavily insured people besides the vessel. She wasn't in deep water, and was sitting straight up. So they sent salvage out there, picked her up and brought her into Miami. Mr. Chapelle looked at her, and later said to me:

"Jim, there wasn't a damn thing wrong with that boat, not a mark on her anywhere. On her forward deck she had a hatch cover that was hinged aft, on the after side, and in this heavy weather some how, some way, the water had broken the toggle out that held that thing down to the fiberglass and carried it away."

They couldn't fasten anything or do anything there, so they had brought all of their mattresses and all of everything and stuffed up underneath of the mattresses to try to keep the sea from pouring in. But as the weight of the water got to the mattresses they couldn't hold them up and this is what they were doing all the Maydaying about. Evidently he never did turn and run with it. Why, nobody knows, but if he had only turned at first and scudded he should have been okay.

Dining Table Setup

In a centerboarder, you generally have the dining table leaves hinged to the centerboard well. If you do that, then the seats along the sides of the cabin have to be close enough so that you can sit at the table when the leaves are up. It takes right much planning to arrange all this so that the setup will be comfortable.

You generally build the seats and then put a back to them that's shoulder high—not as high as your head or you'd be bumping your head when it was rough going. Behind the seats you have your berths, running over to the sides of the boat. You stand up on the cushions of the seats to make up the berths. It's things like this that worries the ladies a lot, but I don't know of any way you can avoid it unless you have such a large boat that you have staterooms or a very wide area where the table would be.

The yachts always have a drawer under the seats down to the cabin sole, but I never have figured out what you do with your feet and legs when you pull the drawer out. I think you're supposed to get on your hands and knees—up in the air backward—and pull the drawer out and look down in it. What works a whole lots better is a hinged front, hinged down to the cabin sole and spring loaded, so that you can pull it down to the cabin sole, put your foot on it and reach back or stuff things in it, and when you take your foot off it flies shut like a mousetrap.

You'll have lots of storage space under the berths. You could lift hatches under the mattresses to get at it, but I think it's easier for the ladies to enter from the side, through panels behind the seat cushions. There they keep their linens and all kinds of things that women bring aboard boats. I have made them with a little bit of of a lip on the forward edge so that you don't find everything pressed hard against the panel when you open it. The woman will usually design this if there's to be a woman aboard. A man

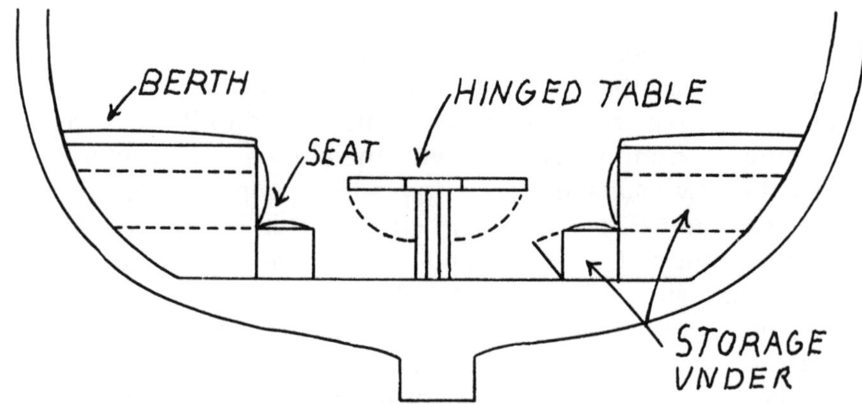

might design something quite different. There's a big sailboat here in the creek that has big lockers on each side of her, about three feet wide, three feet high and five or six feet long and each one holds a pickup truck of beer. Those things are full most of the time. When they finish a sixpack they put the cans back in the things so they can unload them into a dumpster when they come back to port-time was when it was trash overboard downwind as far as the eye could see, but not any more. They sleep on top of those things and it works rather nicely. There's a light overhead and you can lie up there out of the traffic and read. But that boat is not rigged for women at all.

The Galley

This usually goes near your hatch opening, for ventilation. I'll probably get my appliances from a trailer—a three burner propane gas stove and one of those little refrigerators that you can switch over, from gas to 12-volt to shore current.

Head & Shower

Sometimes the best thing is a unit out of a trailer. You have the head in the shower stall and everything is plastic. If the going is rough you can sit on the head and shower yourself and not be bumped all around in there.

Trim

The prettiest trim I every saw was cherry, and I saw a boat up at Lake Champlain that was trimmed in butternut. Mostly mahogany is the accepted plush wood for the finish work of a big boat. I bought four pieces of solid core Africa walnut plywood for the *Norman*. It forms the sides of the shower stall and head, where I needed a clean panel coming and going. That's the only plywood on the boat, other than some drawer bottoms and things like that. I have some panels between the portholes made of yellow pine, standing out about a half inch so I have a place to run wire. Each one has a knot in it just so I can hear the talk.

The quality of a boat is directly in proportion to her *joiner** work. A cheap hull will have fast joiner work and a good hull will have fancy, good quality (if not good taste) joiner work. I did one boat that was designed by an interior decorator from Philadelphia. She had pink formica plastered to everything. She was pink formica crazy. Now that was something, I'll tell you. If you could go into that without a feeling that hit you in the stomach, you had a good digestive system. She was also strong on yellow, but I told her pink and yellow didn't go together. That would certainly make you sick at the stomach.

*Joiner work refers to cabinetry and similar work on a boat, usually interior work.

Ceiling

If you are going to ceil the boat—that is, line the inside to hide the frames, you should leave a half inch space between your ceiling boards. That way you get a good air flow. The floor, or sole or whatever you call it, should be fairly solid and tight, since you're going to have a floor covering over it of some sort. But it will be open to the sides so you get your circulation of cool air from the bilge, which is just naturally the coolest part of the boat.

By all means there should not be any place, anywhere on the boat, completely sealed off. There's a three-cornered place at the stern where the frames and everything meet that I level off with bituminous—roofing filler. If you pour it in when it's red hot and smoking it will seek out the smallest openings and fill up all of those places so no fungi can get in there and start working. Same for the places where everything meets coming down the stem. I've repaired boats there were 15-20 years old and still had the original shavings in those places, wet and rotten. You can imagine what the boat smelled like by and by.

Lights

I though we'd need two lights, one over the table and one in the head. But my son-in-law figured 24. He said there's got to be one over the galley, and one at the head of each berth, and one on the beam running fore and aft at the top of the main cabin, and on and on till we got 24 lights—200 feet of wire.

And of course you have to figure it out so you can run your lights under sail without drawing down your starting battery. I'll probably have an extra generator of some description.

Chapter Six

Getting Her Afloat

As you come near launch time, the first thing you have to do is finish plugging all those nail holes that you have ignored up to now so that you could go on to more interesting work. I cut my own plugs, with a plug cutter, from the same wood as whatever I'm plugging. For the interiors I glue them, but on the outside I bed them in a white lead paste on the decks and topsides, and a red lead paste on the planking. I make up the paste from powders that I had before they made lead illegal.

After you get your plugs in and chiseled off flush, you have to fill all those seams that opened up as the boat dried while you were building her. If you stood on the deck of the *Norman* and looked down into her, it looked like lattice work. I had half-inch openings between some of the planks. If you're not a yachtsman, you take care of this by going to some hardware store and buying a bunch of roof cement. This stuff will stay soft and pliable for 20 years anyhow—that's as long as I've been using it. I've taken it apart after 20 years and it's still pliable. You have to have something to stabilize it like a little bit of oakum, so you put a string of that in and then you plaster in the seams with roof cement. As the boat swells, the cement will squeeze out. She'll compact the oakum, but it won't hurt her as long as you take great care to get the oakum even—not any lumps and bumps in it. When you eventually haul the boat the cement will be standing out two or three inches in some places, and you just cut all that off.

You can use portland cement in the seams of old schooners that are finished swelling—but you'd destroy a new boat with it because it can't give. One time I saw Percy

Todd put a new keel in a *pungy* out of cement. He took out the old rotted inside part with a fire shovel and threw it over her side. He took it down even with the top inside surface of the planking. All those bolts were sticking up from what was left of the old keel. He made himself a form, mixed the cement real rich, poured her full, and trowelled it off. When he took the form off, the cement had picked up the lines of the grain and when he put copper paint on it, it looked exactly like a piece of timber. He made it wide so it caught all of his frames. It was a nice job.

PUNGYS, descended from the Baltimore Clippers, were the first oyster dredging boats on Chesapeake Bay but their keel construction made them less practical than the bugeyes and skipjacks and they were eventually superceded. None are left.

Paint

I think it's foolish to talk much about paint because a lot of people read advertisements and are influenced by what they read. If you're fooling around with boats in the industry like I am you'll use a soft red copper, inside and out. I paint up to the waterline inside with it. It's the best fungicide you can get, and about as cheap as anything else. I also use it on ends and edges of the cabin framing, along with fungicidal bedding, to keep the water from creeping under the roof and destroying her.

I also got 40 pounds of red lead powder for the *Norman*. I mixed it with boiled linseed oil and used it as a thick paint on the bottom. You can't use it in the seams because it gets hard and would burst the edges off the oak as she swelled. But you can put it in other places about an eighth inch thick and you can seal up a right many places with it.

I won't carry a great deal of paint aboard the *Norman* since she will be home based. But she'll have a bunch of boiled oil, a bunch of varnish, and paint of what color is on her—gray and white and copper. That's all she'll have on her other than her red bead. I certainly don't feel any need to work on all that. If I scruff it up it'll be scruffed up till I get back. The gray is on the washboards—the covering boards. The decks will be oiled for the first two or three years. If I ever finish getting on all the oil and all the pitch that they will take, then I'll paint them gray.

I'll try to keep varnish on her rails, but other than that there's very little *bright work* on her. If you don't have anything much to do you can take care of it—but paint lasts longer.

Launch Day

People think you always have to hire house movers to get a big heavy boat into the water, but that's not so. You get a little chain & fall and pull it in. I built the *Norman* in a shady spot a couple hundred feet back from the cove. I put her in on a high tide late in 1982. I didn't have a bit of trouble. I winched her over to the brow of a little hill on wooden rollers. Then I jacked her up till she was even with the top of that brow. I needed the brow because I needed that much down for the slides. When I jacked her up that gave me a chance to get under her and fix her bottom and get her worm shoe and plate underneath of her. A man from a shipyard in Baltimore gave me some nice steel plate to put under her shoe to protect it from groundings. After that I tripped her over onto the skids till the tide was right, and in she went. We didn't wait for the newspapers.

One time I pulled the gunboat *Philadelphia* half the length of the Science & Technology exhibition at the Smithsonian in Washington. She was supposed to weigh 30

tons. We brought it down 90 feet, made a quarter turn and brought it over 60 feet. I didn't know it when I took the job on, but the building inspector had put in there that I couldn't push, pull, pry or jack from any part of the building. He thought he was going to throw me. Still we managed. One man moved her down and turned her while the rest of us went about on other work.

We did use movers on the *Dove* but that was because my back was to the wall. They had invited all those people down and it was going to be touch and go. We had to pull it out of the shed over to where he could begin to dig in with his steel. I pulled it about 120 feet, using rollers of extra-thick three-inch pipe. We used four in tandem, six or eight feet apart, on oak runners, and pulled her with two chain falls. A couple of my helpers walked along holding a prop under each side. They didn't like it—thought I was going to destroy it and this and that. But when you have that many tons on an 18-inch wide keel, as as long as that 18-inch wide is level, she isn't going to fall over. I just pulled the *Norman* without any props.

The mover had the *Dove* airborne for 20 minutes. He backed over the railway cattybyson and eased her down. He got her lined up perfect on the railway in an hour and a half, and it took him half a day to get his steel out. It cost me $4,000. I couldn't do that with the *Norman*. I don't have that kind of money. It would pay for my sails.

Ballast

Ballast stabilizes your hull. It's the pendulum that offsets the weight of the wind and the rig—in other words it keeps the boat from turning over when you put the sail up. It also enables you to trim the way she rides on the water, and to a degree correct some mistakes you may have made in placement of sails and rigging. By moving ballast forward or aft you can affect her handling to an extent, though nothing radical.

The ballast goes in after you have her in the water and swelled. Lead is the best, everybody will agree. But it's expensive. Iron is a poor second best. Yachsmen paint it to stop it from rusting, but in a boat like mine a little iron oxide in the bilge won't excite anyone. The best iron ballast is the old-fashioned window weight—yet with all the old houses they're tearing down in Baltimore you can't get a window weight to save your soul. You dip the window weight in water two or three times, then roll it in dry cement and lay it out to dry. You may have to do this several times but it will keep the window weight from rusting up the bilge for years. It is the very best iron ballast I know of and you can break it off to whatever lengths you want.

I needed eight tons of ballast for the bugeye. I managed to find some chain. I didn't care if it came out of a warship 100 pounds to the link, just so it could conform to the bottom of the boat. If it comes to putting railroad track in there you have to cut it all into 14-inch pieces and it is much harder on the planking. Also you have to lay strips of wood so that the water can run under them freely. You don't have to do that with chain.

Stones don't have any weight. You can get marble that's very dense heavy stone, but even crushed marble leaves a lot of voids. I put 20 tons of marble in the boat we did for Charleston.

The only ballast you put in a skipjack if you build her right is a little trim ballast aft. Belgian blocks are good—it's the heaviest cut stone you can get without paying a lot of money.

I put 20 tons of cobble stones in the *Dove*. They took them out and used them in their park restoration and put iron bars in her in place. They saved a fortune on that.

Chapter 7

Spars and Rigging

When you get the boat overboard you're not finished by right much. I think that the spars and their rig—to make them up and rig them is probably pretty close to a quarter of the work and expense and fuss and muss to doing the boat.

I'm talking about hours. By the time you start out with your mast and booms or gaffs or what and get those things properly made and installed and wedged up and then do the standing and running rigging, you're going to be involved in a right many hours, especially if you want nice work and Lord knows you wouldn't want to put a lot of time on a boat and then rush through that part. The satisfacion of a boat has a lot to do with the ease of handling it. If it's going to kill you to handle it then you have what a lot of people think a sailboat calls for—a lot of work. But it's not true. If the rig is properly made and properly installed and properly balanced, it's a *pleasure* to sail a sailboat. But if it's not, then it's work all the way.

Mast Materials

As far as spars are concerned, I'm sure most everybody is agreed that the mast itself, if you are going to get the very best, would be spruce. Sitka spruce from Alaska is the finest, but the Japanese are taking all of that for pulpwood. Nowadays we have to be satisfied with fir or black spruce or some other material that comes next best to hand. A yellow pine mast will last a long time. Our fathers put yellow pine masts in them that lasted 40-50 years. Cedar makes a good light mast for a small yacht but it won't take abuse. We have a mast laying here in the yard that came from an old boat down at James Island, the *Collier;* it was the largest skipjack on the Bay. She had a cyprus mast in her and it must have gone all of her lifetime and now it's going to be chopped for another boat. So you don't have to let your spars go if you use native wood. They just have to be taken care of like anything else. We used cyprus on the *Dove* because it was available at the time, and so far as lasting is concerned it is superior. But it's not every time you can lay your hands on that type of cyprus, or cyprus that's big enough for a large boat's mast. If you put in a cyprus mast, you make it an inch thicker than you do if you're putting in a spruce mast. Cyprus doesn't have the shear strength that sitka spruce has.

I think yellow pine is as strong as spruce until you get up into the head of it where the knots occur. When you get there you're going to come down in shear strength right much. All the big pines have all of their limbs in the tops of them and when you're after an 80-foot pole you are going to run into big knots in the top and that's all there is to it. The same thing can occur in cyprus. But you take black spruce that comes down from Maine—they have little limbs all the way up in them. They don't have big tops so of course you don't have the problem. I've got one in the yard that's 70 feet and there isn't any knot in there that's two inches across, whereas if you had a 75 or 80 foot yellow pine mast you'd have knots in there that would be three or four inches across—unless you were going straight up out of the heart. But it's highly unlikely that you would get a piece so straight that you could just use the heart.

The masts for the bugeye are 55 feet and 53 feet. I'm rigging her short. If she was for a young man they'd be a few feet longer. I'd put 60 feet and 58 feet in it if I didn't mind fooling and reefing and all that kind of thing.

The largest spar I ever chopped, on the *Constellation,* wound up to be 33 inches through it. It took five people five weeks to chop the first 75 feet on that. To chop the next 25 feet was a lot of touch and go because the pole was too small to make what they required. It was light chopping from then on.

Nowadays there's only a few mills around that will handle long stuff. We have to go clear to Chestertown to find a mill that would run 45-50 feet. We don't have any that would run you 80 feet. I think the lathe they have at Mystic, Connecticut, will produce 75 feet or something like that. A lathe that they have on the West Coast will run 90 feet because the poles we got for the *Boston Pilot* were 95 feet. They were lathed all but a big clump on one end. I think they couldn't get straight what we wanted. We wanted a square top to the masts on our schooner so we could get the cross trees and trestle trees on them. So they just left us a great big lump on the end of those things 10 feet long and we had to chop it by hand.

Chopping It Out

By the time you transport a piece of mast stock back and forth to the mill that has a carriage long enough to run it, you better chop it. Everybody groans when you talk about it, but if you'd count the time, let alone the expense, I think you'd come off as fast chopping as running all over the state looking for a mill.

When you chop, the first thing you do is make your log four square. After you get her four square you go eight. After the eight it's 16 before you begin to round the spar. On the *Constellation*'s spar we went to 32 before beginning to round. It's impossible to round from a square or anything like that.

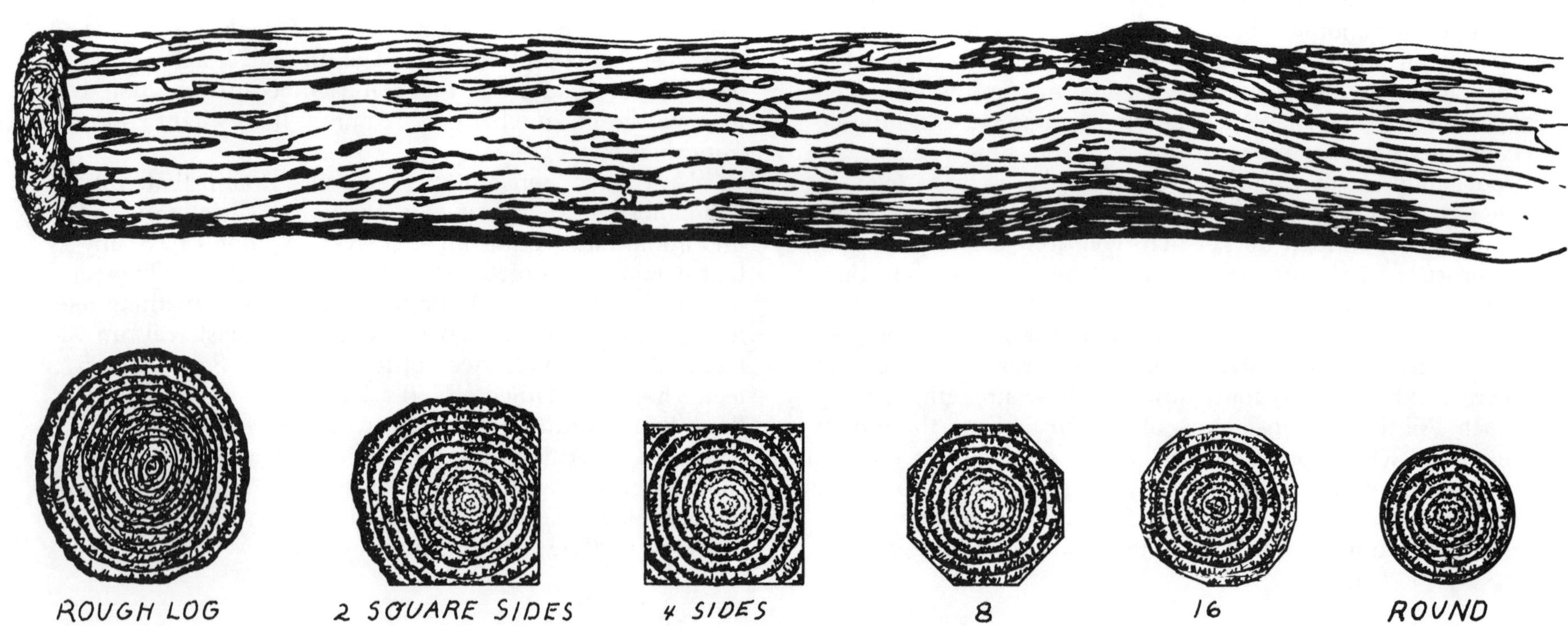

Your first cut is flat. If you're careful, and the stick will allow it, you can run right straight up and take all your measurements off that flat side. You don't start by jumping up on top of it and chopping like our fathers did. Instead, you score in every two feet or so with a chain saw. Then you split the blocks off in between the scoring with a broad axe. Then you take a foot adze or house carpenter's adze, whatever you want to call it, and work that back. And of course you have to have a lip adze to finish it out. By then you are coming off with a very smooth piece of wood that looks almost like it was dressed. You get it straighter and straighter with every face you cut, and if your people have been careful, and haven't cut too deep anywhere, or sawed too deep with the chain saw, it begins to look like a lathed piece of wood.

If you lay off your mast according to the plans in all the "how to build" books you're going to have a straight taper. That bothers you some because it always looks hollow. I never use that formula unless I'm just roughing in. I always let a good mast swell a little about a third of the way up and then begin to come back in again so it won't look skinny in the middle and spread out on the ends. In order to carry the gaff and top sails, a schooner's mast will draw in a whole lot less at the top than a jib-headed rig.

People wonder why the masts on Chesapeake Bay boats rake aft. Well, that apparently began so that the halyard block would come smack dab over the center of the cargo hold. It was for loading and unloading. Some dredgers think the boom lays off better in light air if the mast hangs aft. But all of the new skipjacks have their masts standing straighter than the old ones. I never did put a lot of rake in them. I always stood them fairly straight and I've had very good luck with them.

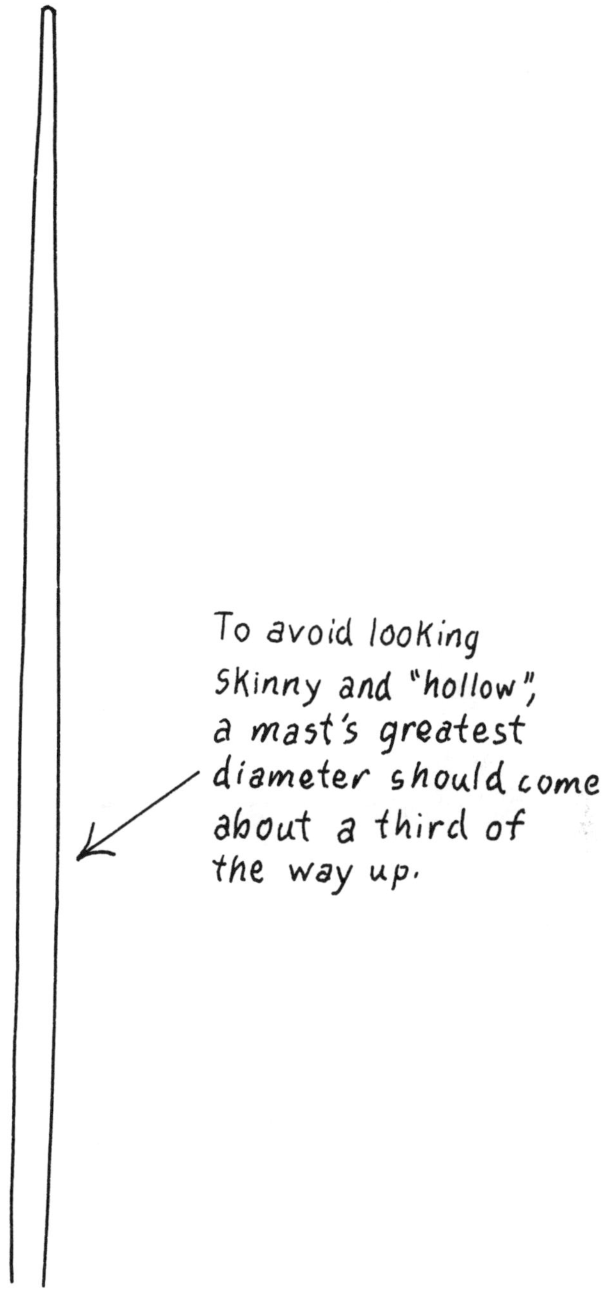

Booms

For the booms on a yacht you can usually get square timber from the mill. The only trick to making a boom is to keep the underneath side of it perfectly straight and work all of the shape into the top and sides of it. That way, when you hang it and it sags and the weight of the sail comes on it you will come out with a pretty straight-looking boom.

Finish

To preserve the masts and booms you should give them as much oil as they will take—boiled linseed oil. You can go with palm oil or other things but you have to be careful not to use anything that will stain a spar if you're going to let it stay bright. A painted spar on a skipjack would be an abomination. It's almost an abomination on anything. Second after that is a varnished spar—but you can't say that; if you did you'd have yachtsmen down your throat until you choke to death. They'd smother you out.

Rigging—Making It Simple

When it comes to rigging, a work schooner and a schooner-rigged yacht are worlds and worlds apart. They are so radically different that you are just not talking about the same thing. Let's start off with what we had in the Bay—schooners that went everywhere. One of them, less than 100 feet, went to California through the Straits of Magellan. When she got to California she heard there was plenty of freight out of Australia—and somebody in California wanted to send something to Australia. So he picked up this load and he ran it to Australia. In Australia he picked up a load and ran it somewhere over by India. When he discovered where he was, he came on around the other way—he sailed the bloody thing all the way around. When he got home he was wore out—the running rig and everything like that had to be redone—but he had made for her owners a handsome profit from these long voyages, which is generally not what you do with a small centerboard schooner.

That boat had on her, for running rigging, halyards—the throat and peak halyards—on each of her masts. She had sheets on her jib and her fore and main sails. There was not a sign of a winch *anywhere* on her. There wasn't anything mechanical at all except to get the anchor. Now can you imagine a yacht going anywhere without, you know, a lot of wire, a lot of winches, a lot of backstays, a lot of all kinds of strange things? So, you can rig simple or you can rig complicated, and the more complicated they are, the more you are supposed to have on them to make them easy to handle. But I'm sure of one thing, you muddy the water on a schooner yacht with all of this gear. You really, really don't need it.

When I was a boy I helped a little bit at the Cambridge shipyard where we dismantled the Conway fleet—took the masts out and got 'em ready for engines. The *Grace May* was 120 feet on her deck, which is a right large schooner. She had two masts in her. She had a deck engine and that engine was there for three things. One was to get the anchor. Another was to assist the loading and unloading of cargo. The third thing that it did, they had lines that led to the—I can't call it what they called it—but anyhow they had winch heads that stuck out on each side of the donkey engine. They had the mate on one side carrying the throat halyard, and the deckhand on the other carrying the peak halyard. Each one watched what he was doing. And that engine set that mainsail with those two winch heads. It was the only mechanical thing on that schooner, and three men ran her all the time: the captain, the mate, and the deckhand who was the cook. If the captain was going to go way down in the Caribbean he might take a man aboard to serve as navigator, but it would be unusual, and wouldn't have anything to do with the handling of the vessel. So they were rigged extremely simple and they did very well with her.

I would think that two people would be ample for a 40-foot schooner with gaff-rigged sails—but you would have to have at least two people. It wouldn't be a handy rig for the two, for the plain and simple reason that whenever you wanted to shorten sail you would have to take the man away from the wheel to let down. You can't just let the throat down a way, then let the peak down a way, then the throat and so forth. You can't be doing that unless you've got all day, and if you're letting down to reef you have got to let down. One man can't handle both of the halyards because they run at a different pace. However, you could do it with yourself and your wife if it was a light rig with light gaff and light line. You could lead one of the halyards aft so that one of you could stand at the wheel and assist without leaving the steering.

I have a friend ready to do a large ferro-cement boat which is designed to sail anywhere, any time. Both masts are gaff-rigged, and he's planning on going alone for the better part of the time. I was worried until he came and asked me to make the jaws for his gaffs. I discovered that these were three inches through at the jaws. So we're just hoisting little sticks. There's no reason in the world why a man can't do that. These gaffs and booms are light and expendable, but I would whole lots rather have a pole I could hoist and break one out once in a while than have one I couldn't hoist.

Standing Rigging

Most of the standing rigging—fixed rigging you don't have to fool with while you're sailing along—on a 40-foot schooner would be half-inch galvanized wire. You have a *jib stay*, or *forestay*, which is possibly the heaviest piece of wire on the boat, and this would be three-quarters inch. This runs from the *hounds* of the foremast out close to the end of the bowsprit. It goes down through a beehole in the bowsprit, turns back and is caught to one end of a turnbuckle. The other end of the turnbuckle is fastened to the highest of the *bob chains* just above the waterline of the boat.

Forward of the jib stay, you have a half-inch piece, called a *head stay*, that runs to the head of the mast. This would likely fasten to a collar on the bowsprit, with a wire underneath running to the lower bob chain. If the boat is a two-topmast schooner, that is if she has a top on the foremast, there would be a wire running from the top of that out to the end of the jib boom, and that would be braced underneath by wires to the *dolphin-striker* or *martingale*, which is a pole pointing straight down from the underside of the bowsprit.

Coming back, you would have a *triatic* stay, tying the heads of the two masts together. Then you'd have a stay from the top of the main topmast down to the head of the foremast to hold the main topmast from going back or whatever. If you use a foretopsail, it has to be thrown over that wire every time you go about, so it isn't used unless you are in the trade winds, or coming up the Chesapeake with the winds out of the southwest or something like that so that you could be running for many hours without changing it.

A schooner will have two pieces of wire that go to the hounds of each mast, on each side, and another one to the top of the topmast, so there will be three stays altogether—*shrouds* you call them—on each side. That's all there is—there won't be any backstays or after stays, although there generally is a wire running down from the hounds on each side to the middle of the main boom. These would serve as a *topping lift*, which keeps the whole mess off the deck when the sail is down. The *lazy jacks* would be rigged to the two wires. They catch the sail as you lower it.

All the wire in the world won't help you sometimes. The *Pride of Baltimore* brought up several hundred gallons of water in the jib folds in a storm early in 1981. The jib stay snapped. It couldn't stand the weight. They didn't lose their foretopmast until that night or the next day. It was there without any stay and it snapped out. I suppose that they were afraid to send anybody out to make the end of the thing fast jury rigged. I don't know why they weren't running with the storm anyhow. The engine's too little to push her into it. They paid half as much for putting the engine in that boat as we got for building the *Dove*.

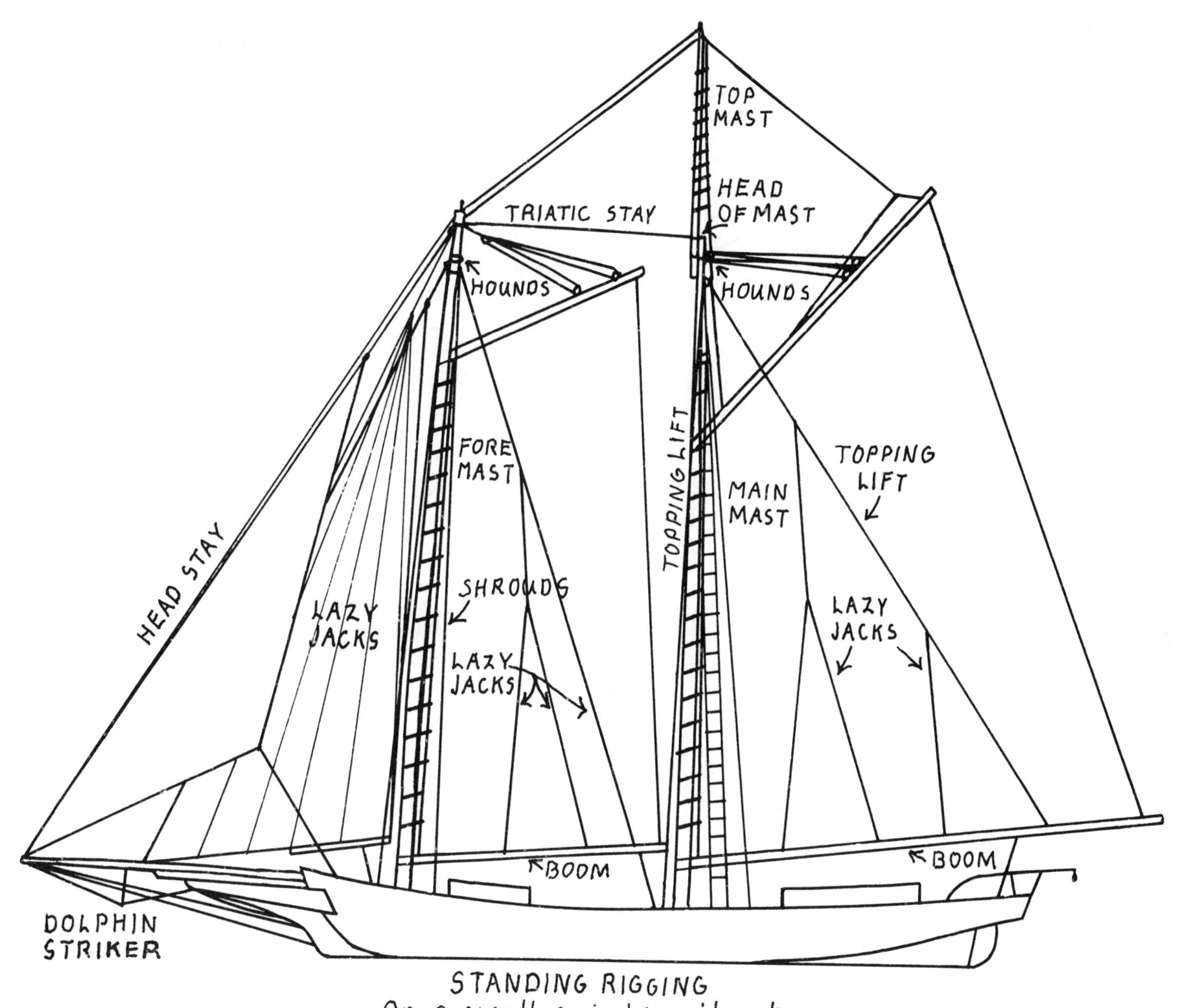

STANDING RIGGING
On a small main topsail schooner

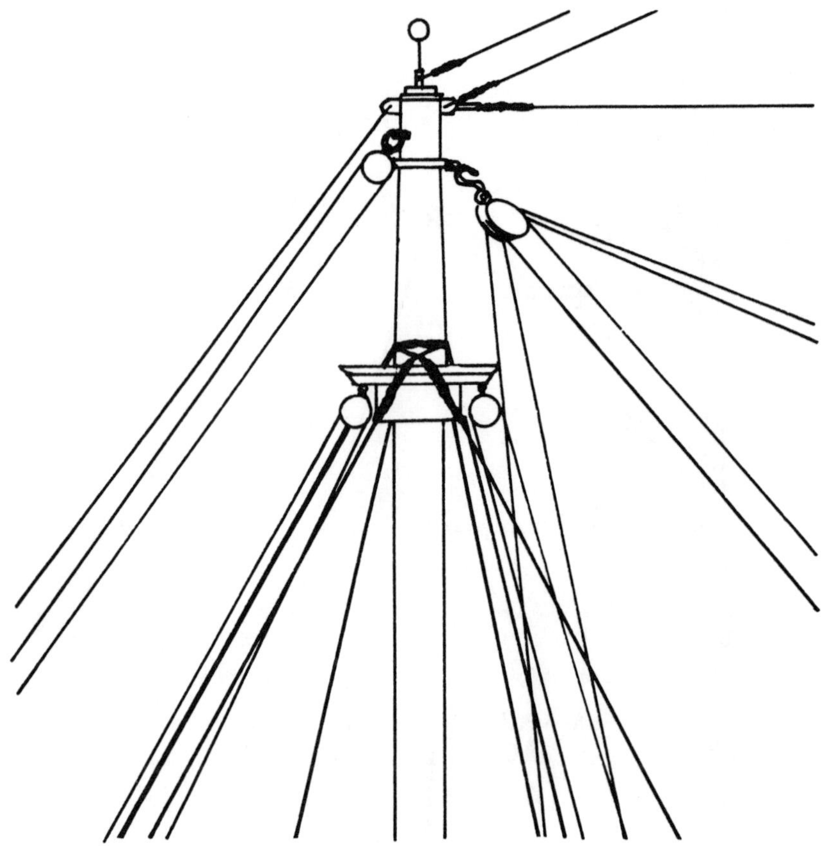

The stays wrap around the mast and get seized there. Each end comes on down — unless you have a fancy yacht rigger. He makes it up in separate pieces puts a loop in every piece. That makes twice as many wraps at the hounds of the mast... makes an ugly bundle that dosn't serve any purpose.

I'll turn up my wires like the old timers did. I wouldn't use any stainless. First it would be out of the question with me because I don't have that kind of money. Second it would be out of character on the boat. If you use stainless you can use a lot smaller wire and still get the same strength. But you're always in trouble with your ends. I know there are plenty of people in the world that can splice stainless wire, but they're not readily available. Stainless just doesn't lend itself for standing rigging.

The traditional way of doing it is to take the wire around the *deadeye* and make it as tight as you can and wrap it—*seize* it—with wire for two or three inches. They had a regular soft wire just for it. Then you wrap it with marline—*serve* it—or you *parcel* it first, wrap it with canvas and tar the whole mess, and then come on with marline. Every four or five years they made some adjustments until the rigging was finally set, with the *lanyards* the right height off the deck. So you don't *want* the deadeyes spliced to the stays. A lot of people can't splice anyways. They just stuff it in and beat it down; stuff it in and beat it down. If you want to see wire spliced you've got to go down to Norfolk and Cape Charles and see some of those old chaps about my age. They do it so smooth.

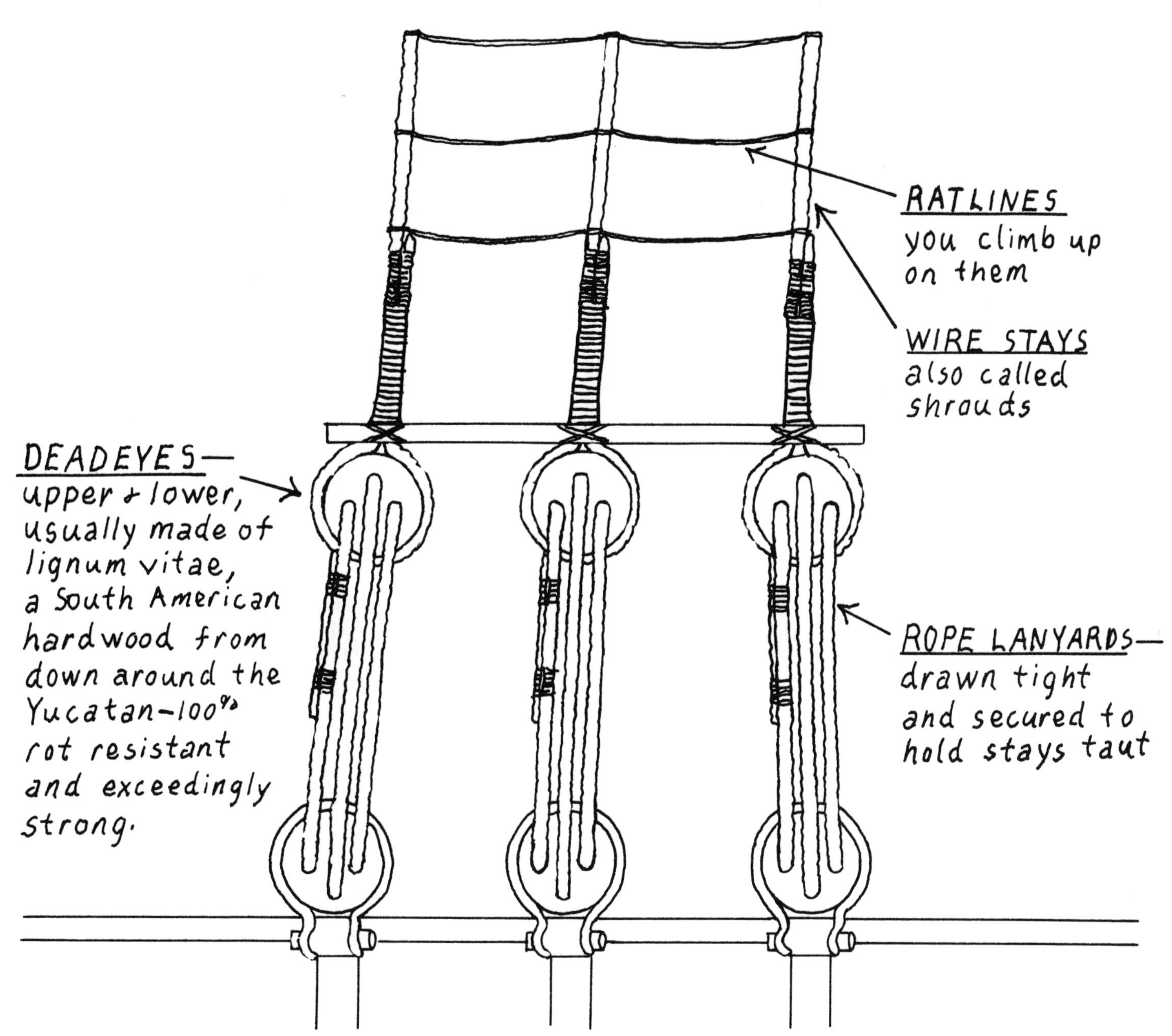
RATLINES
you climb up on them
WIRE STAYS
also called shrouds
DEADEYES—
upper + lower, usually made of lignum vitae, a South American hardwood from down around the Yucatan–100% rot resistant and exceedingly strong.
ROPE LANYARDS—
drawn tight and secured to hold stays taut

PARCEL: Take a strand of oakum and put it between the layers of the rope to make it round (called worming) then you wrap with canvas and tar the mess.

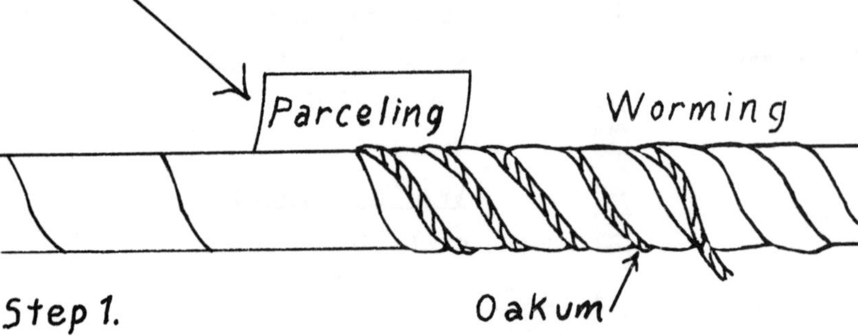

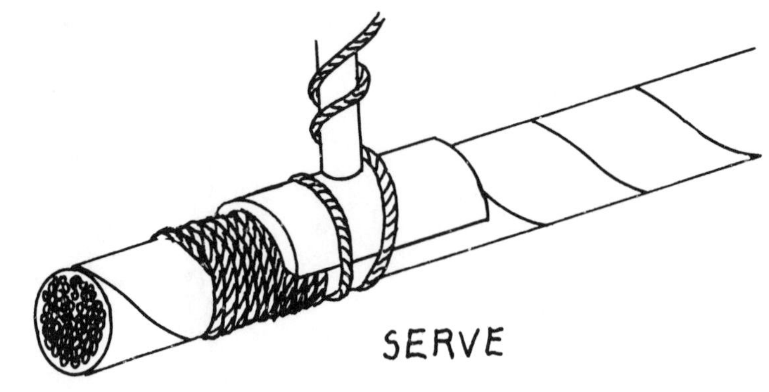

Step 2

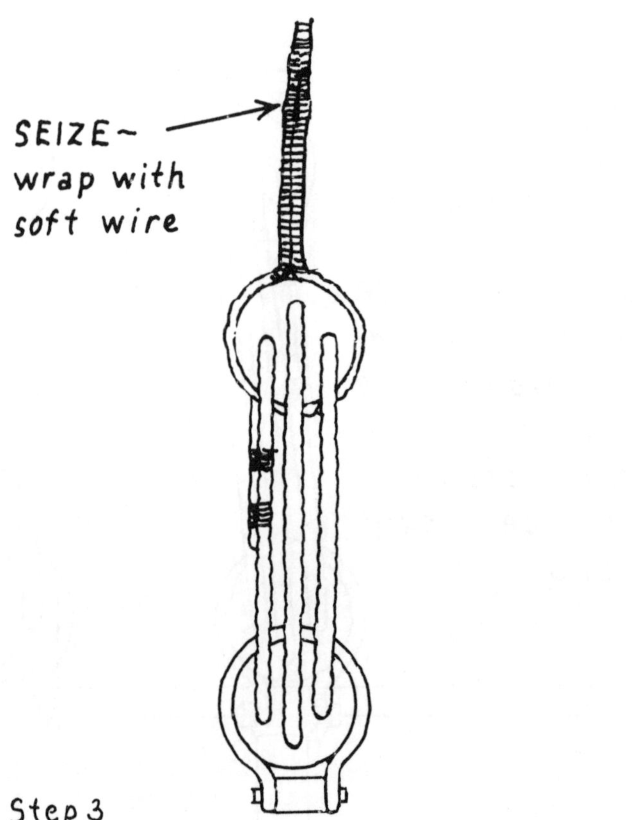

Step 3

Blacksmithing

There's no blacksmith around that we know of—certainly fewer than a half-dozen on the East Coast, that know anything about marine blacksmithing. If anybody went to a regular standard inland blacksmith he would have to have exact dimensions of what he wanted and he would have to have the name of a place where he could get it galvanized—otherwise it would run iron rust all over him all of the time. If he had a good blacksmith and precise dimensions or drawings it wouldn't make any difference where he was—they can make anything.

We got two tons of iron from Easton Steel for the *Boston Pilot*. We used the whole two tons to fabricate the stuff up her masts—great bands made out of 5/8 thick stuff four and five inches wide, eyebolts an inch and a quarter in diameter, cranes made of inch and a half bar, the greatest mess you ever saw. We had a blacksmith come up from Savannah; he had himself all written up, what a great forge artist he was, and he had business cards and all. When he saw what I wanted he pretty near fainted. He had made iron gate hinges and the like. We had pieces of iron that would upend him over the top of his anvil. He charged me two days travel time plus the one day he stayed. I got him to make me two rings. My helper and I did all the rest.

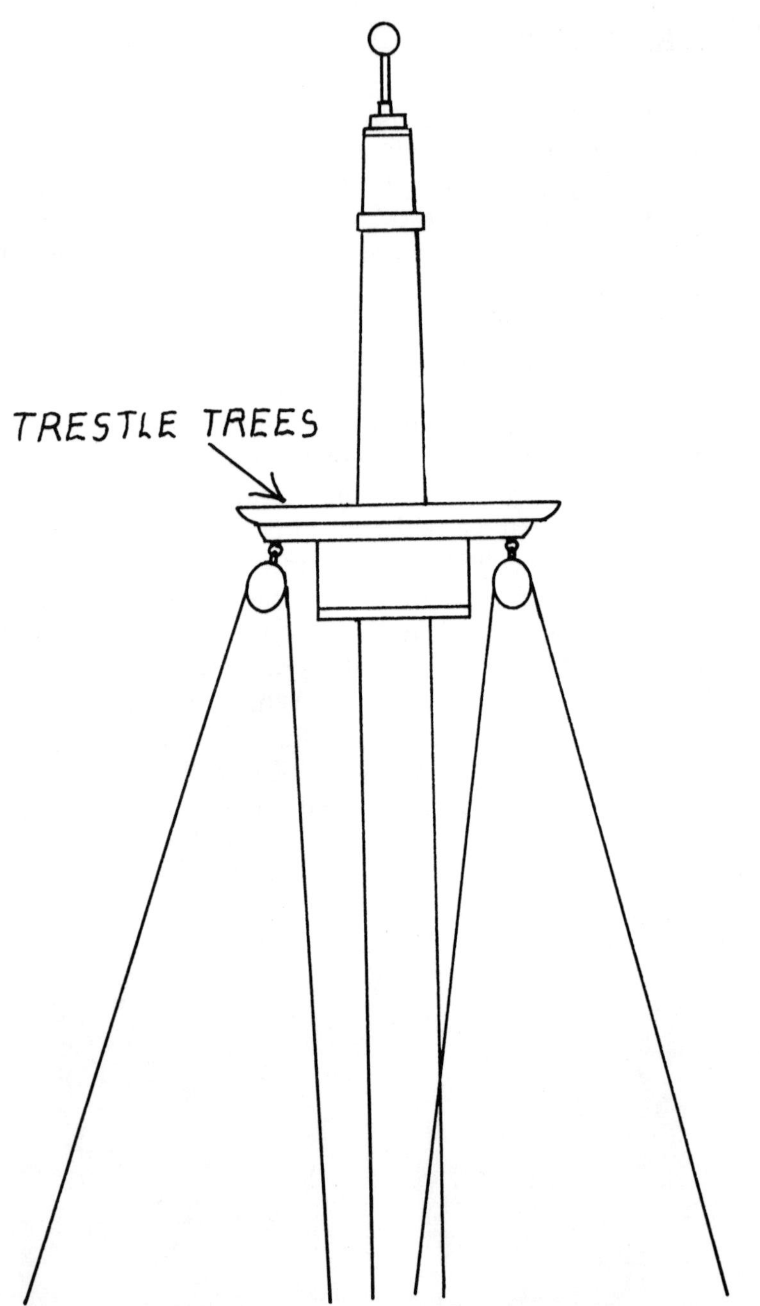

Running Rigging

You'll have a throat and peak *halyard* on each mast for hoisting the gaff sails. You'll also have halyards for raising the topsail and the two jibs. You'll have *sheets* to let you control the two gaff sails and the jibs while you move along. You'll have *downhauls* to help you bring down the sails that you can't get out and pull on with your hands—the jibs, the topsail. You'll have *clewlines* and an *outhaul* to help you set and take in the topsail.

You use dacron rope for your sheets and halyards nowadays and keep it from chafing so it will last. Hardly anybody uses manila any more.

To keep the halyards from chafing on a schooner you have a set of *trestle trees* up there made of oak. You hang your throat halyard on one side and your peak halyard on the other, and those pieces of oak stand forward and aft and have these eyes with the blocks hanging from them, out far enough that they don't beat and scratch against the mast.

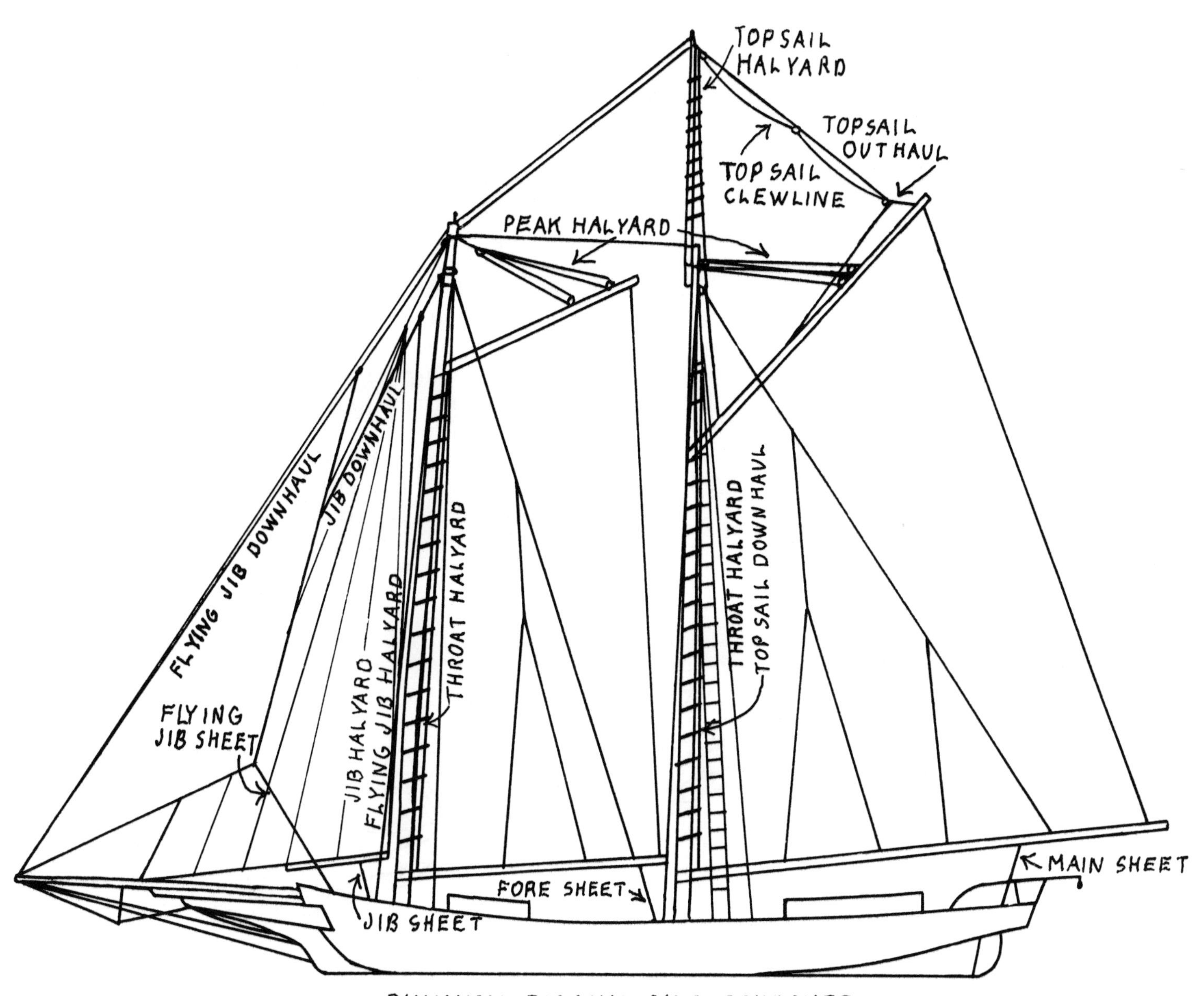

RUNNING RIGGING ON A SCHOONER
ALL LINES LEAD TO DECK

On a boat, it's always nice if you can make the jib tend itself when you come about, so you don't have to run up there or fool with the sheets. Our Bay workboats were made self-tending by running the sheet up through a block at the hounds of the mast. From where you stood and handled it, the sheet went up to a block at the rail, then over to this ugly thing that rode the *traveler*. It had two sheaves—pulley wheels—in it and it looked like a cucumber. The wheels were cocked at different angles. The sheet went through the one wheel, up the mast to a sheave at the hounds, down the mast to the other wheel, and out to the jib. The whole apparatus had to be fairly light so it wouldn't fall over and defeat it's purpose. It enabled all that line to clear the samson post and so forth so that you could leave the jib sheet alone when you were tacking back and forth into the wind. With your main sheet made fast also, you didn't need to touch anything, just stand at the wheel and steer. I'd recommend it but you have to remember that you'll need to pay for another 100 feet of line, compared to a sheet that just runs out there and snags on the samson post a lot of the time.

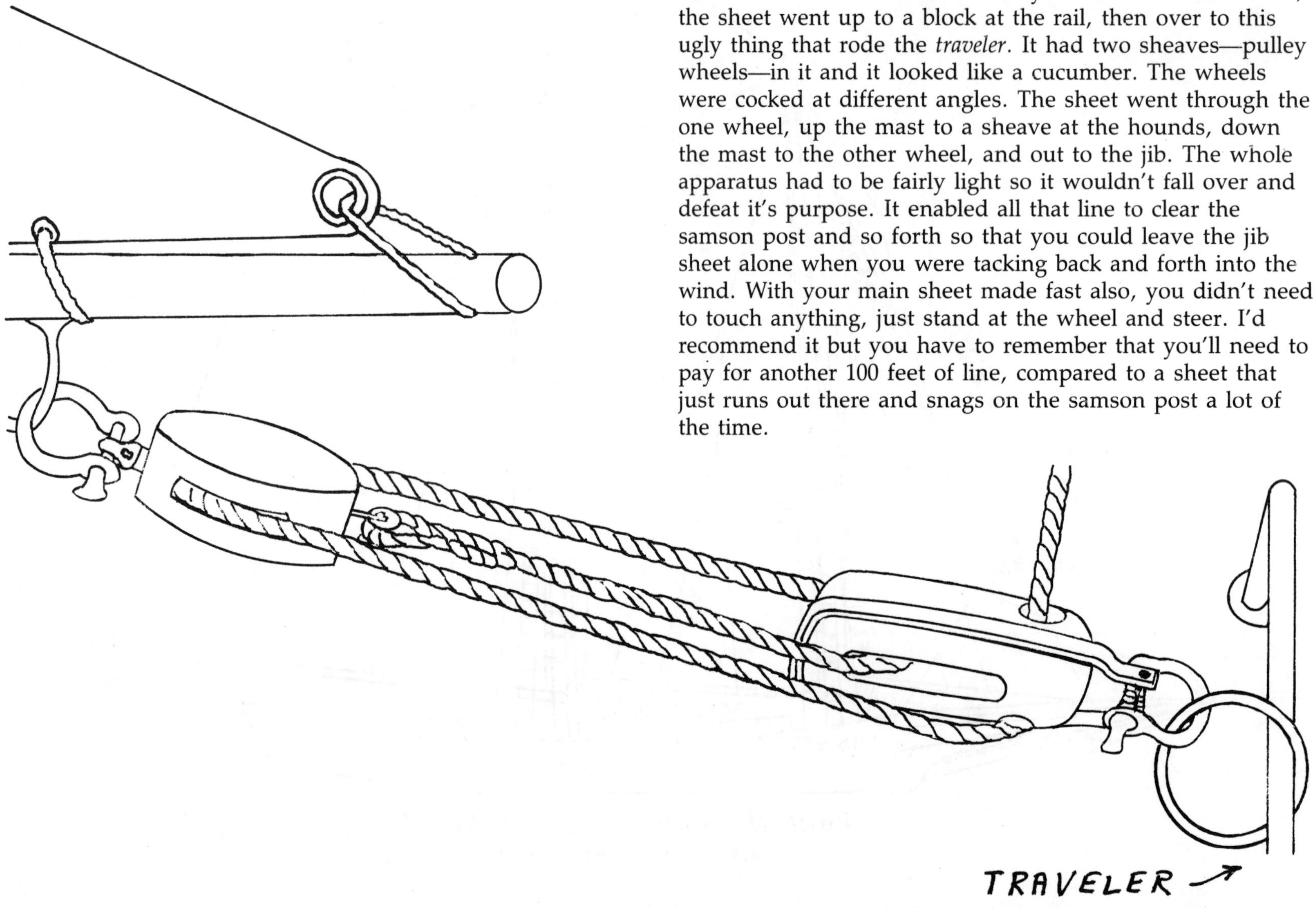

TRAVELER →

If you have a very heavy rig, or you are very light, or you've had a heart attack or something, you can rig a *teacle* to help you get the boom up off the saddle. That's pronounced "teecle" and its just a corruption of tackle. You haul as far as you can on your halyard till your sail is pretty well up but nothing's tight and still the thing weighs as much as you do even with your mechanical advantage. At that point you make your halyard down and get hold of your teacle and pull on that to finally pick the boom up off the saddle.

With a teacle you are pulling a block and fall *with* a block and fall. Ordinarily, you have the end of your halyard making down to a becket on your lower block. To rig a teacle, you just take that end off, put an eye in it, let it hang down with the rigging at the side of the boat to 10 or 12 feet above the deck and hook a little block and fall to it right there. That's a teacle.

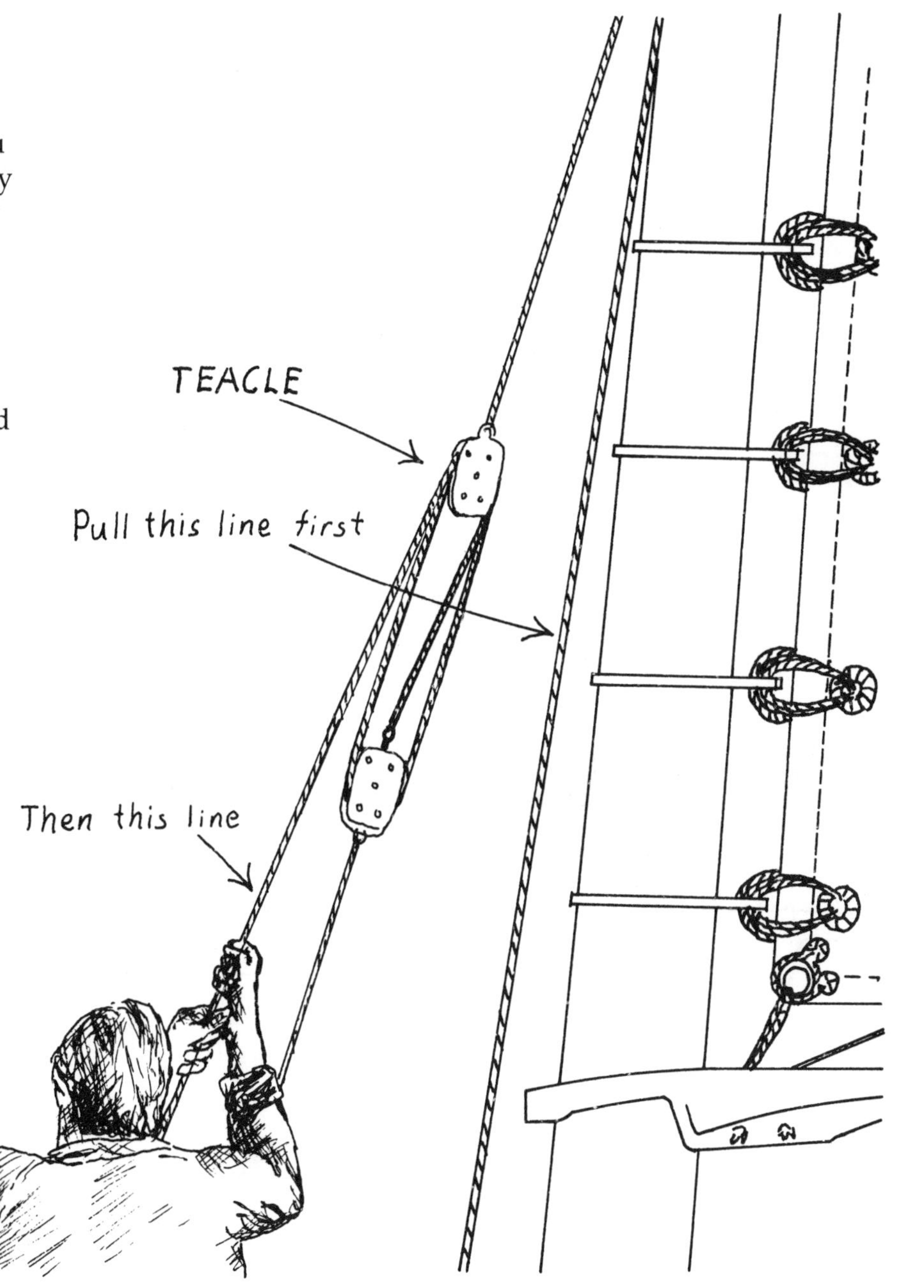

Sails

Sails are a job for a professional. And as much as the material costs nowadays it would be foolish for anybody to presume that he could make a sail that would be worth anything unless he was a sailmaker. I used to make the hoops for hanging them but I don't even do that any more. They take a lot of time and they are very, very difficult to make. You can make them up from strips of very straight grain oak, or ash will take a boiling and bend good. I used to make them in one piece, with the ends riveted. But there

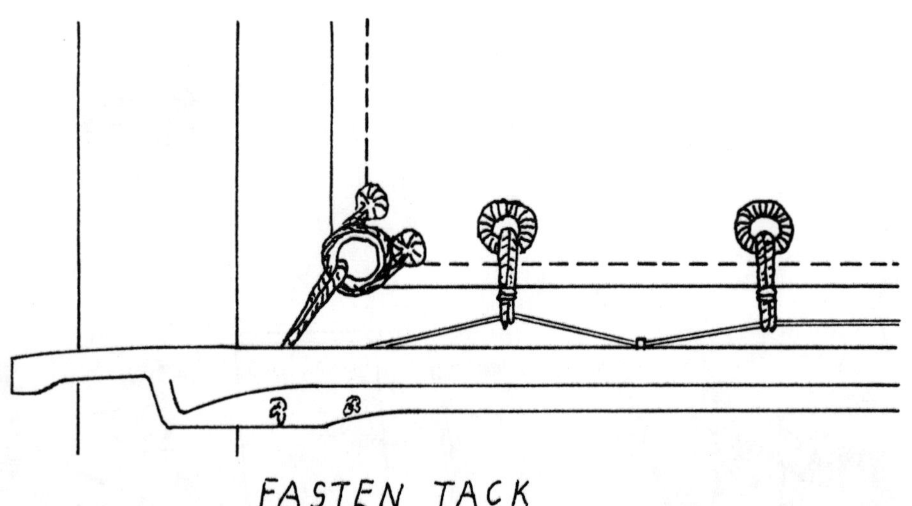
FASTEN TACK

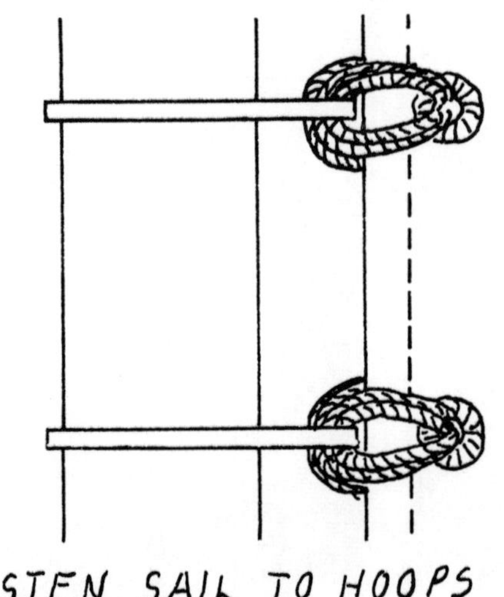
FASTEN SAIL TO HOOPS

would be one place weaker than the other and after a year or two they would get egg-shaped. I have even seen them triangular.

I know of only one man on the East Coast who makes hoops now and that's Pert Lowell from around Mystic.

When you get your sails and your hoops and everything together, the masts stepped and rigging on, then you tie on the sail, or *bend* it on as they say. It's not difficult. Almost every sail has a *head* and a *foot*. Usually the foot attaches to a boom (otherwise it's called a loose-footed sail), and the head is brought up by a halyard, or two halyards in the case of a gaff sail. You generally have an *outhaul* at the out end of a boom to keep the foot taut. Jibs are normally fastened to the forestay with snaps. You can get this all worked out in a few days, and then you're ready for your first trial under sail. And if you've done well, and gotten it right by and large, you're starting into something you can enjoy for many, many years.

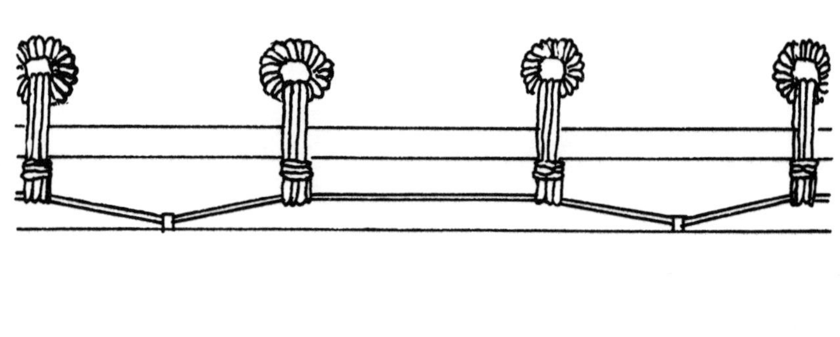

FASTEN SAIL TO BOOM

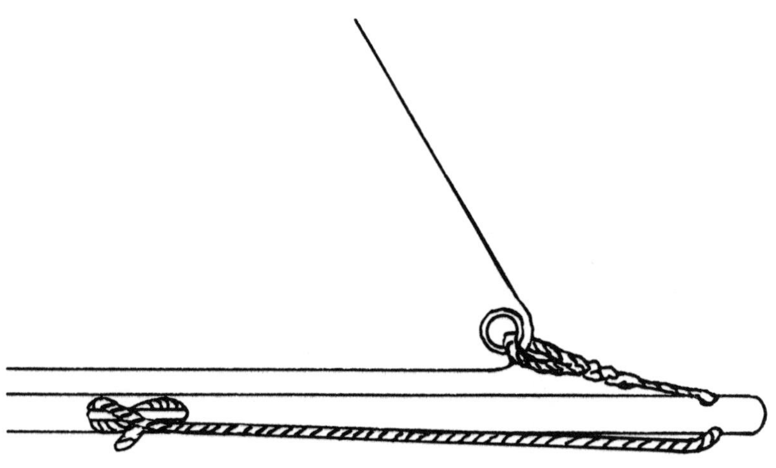

OUTHAUL ON CLEW

The anchor heaves, the ship swings free,
The sails swell full. To sea, to sea!

—Thomas Lovell Beddoes

An Appreciation...

When you sail any distance on Chesapeake Bay, you eventually come across one or two of the rugged old skipjacks still used for the dredging of oysters. You recognize them in a second, even from a couple miles away, because of the tall raking mast. You can be sailing out from the shore and there will be that pine pole sticking out above some cove, with a 10-15 degree lean to it. And you know if you head toward it you will soon see a relic from the past, a boat that's maybe 50, 60, 70 years old, at least the basic parts of it.

Like many others who sail on the Chesapeake, I long ago became enamored with the skipjack: beamy, comfortable, sturdy, hardly any draft in the water to hold you back from exploring the vast shallow parts of the Bay, and at the same time a fine sailing boat and one of the handsomest creations man has ever set to water.

My first thought was to find one of the old boats and convert it to pleasure, as several people have done. But it didn't take much poking and prodding to realize that, as an investment, most of these old-timers should be left to finish out their days in the oyster fleet, where they can earn back their upkeep every year. Besides, I could see that the sail and anchor of these big old vessels could be cumbersome for two people to deal with and almost impossible for one.

It was my quest for a skipjack in sound condition and of a size I could handle that led me, in 1964, to Jim Richardson.

When I first visited his yard, Jim was building a little skipjack (*Sweepstakes*) for Howard Chapelle, the wooden boat historian. Mr. Chapelle had a home in nearby Church Creek, and visited Jim frequently. I knew I was in good company, so far as finding a boatbuilder.

JIM RICHARDSON

Jim and I had some conversations about the layout and decided on a 28-footer. That's the hull, and doesn't count about ten feet of hefty bowsprit that gives a real thrill to the boat, both in looks and action.

The order was placed in the fall, and the boat was ready by next spring. In those days Jim was doing one or two pleasure boats a year, in between repairs and other yardwork, much of it for the dredging fleet. At Jim's suggestion, we named her *Champion Girl,* after an oyster pirate boat that once roamed the lower Potomac River (although in fact her size put her in company with the old crab-scrapers that served the Bay soft crab industry, rather than the larger oyster boats). Jim carved the name on elaborate cedar trailboards, festooned with star-studded patriotic emblems that I later dressed up with paint and gold leaf. As a finishing touch he carved a stunning four-inch figurehead, as full forward as the boat was fine, complete with two red dots.

Champion Girl

The first time I took *Champion Girl* for a test sail I plunged her bowsprit into the Chrysler automobile family's boathouse on the other side of Jim's creek. The boat hadn't responded when I pulled on her tiller. Then I realized the problem: her centerboard hadn't had time to soak up water; it was floating in the well, not doing a bit of good in helping the boat maneuver herself across the wind. I quickly found a mop handle to jam the board down, and I didn't stab the boathouse any more that day.

Other than that mop handle, I never had to add anything or do anything functional to *Champion Girl* from the time Jim turned her out of his yard. Once I got a feel of the sails, got to know the right adjustments of the lines, I could manage the tiller with one or two fingers even in a good breeze. With moderate wind/sea conditions, and the sails set right, I found I could (and still can) "let Jim Richardson sail the boat," that is, take my hand off the tiller and let her tack off on her own, while I lie back and doze till it comes time for the next tack—a boat in perfect balance, and in perfect harmony with the wind and water of Chesapeake Bay.

* * *

In the years since, Jim has taken on some prestigious customers, and the quality of his craftmanship has become known to wooden boat people throughout the world. Every year or so something happens at the yard interesting enough to bring in reporters and TV cameras.

In the early 1970s the city of Charleston, S.C., as part of its tricentennial celebration, called on Jim to build a replica of a 60-foot coastal trading ketch used by Lord Ashley in the 1600s. The *Adventurer* was put on public display at the Charles Towne Landing exhibition park.

Jim turned out an even more ambitious replica ship in 1978, the *Dove*, for St. Mary's City across the Bay. The 60-foot pinnace also became a public attraction, and has graced the cover of sailing magazines in the United States and Europe (as well as the 1983 Baltimore telephone directory).

One time when I visited Jim's yard there was a huge log near his workshop, nearly man-high and 120 feet long. I was told that it had been brought to the docks in Oregon on two railroad cars, carried to Baltimore by ship, dumped into the Bay, towed to Jim's yard by the Coast Guard, and dragged ashore by bulldozer and farm tractors. Under Jim's guidance, a crew of five young workers hewed it by hand into a replacement mast for Baltimore's famous old wooden naval ship, the U.S.F. *Constellation*.

On another visit I found Jim across the road from his place, building a working replica of an old Eastern Shore windmill for State Sen. George Radcliffe. The replica mill replaced one that had been owned by Radcliffe's father and was lost in the blizzard of 1888. The mill, with a wingspan of about 65 feet, is now marked as an historic attraction on Maryland highway maps.

Since his "retirement" in 1973, and in between other projects like the *Dove*, Jim has undertaken a boat for himself, the *Jenny Norman*, a scaled-down 48-foot pleasure version of a bugeye called the *Norma* that plied Chesapeake Bay around the turn of the century. The bugeye was a two-masted, round-hulled craft used in dredging and transport of oysters. Few are left under sail today. Jim refers to the *Jenny Norman* a number of times in this book since its construction is similar in many ways to the wooden schooner proposed. He had the vessel—a master shipwright's dream—nearly completed as this book went to press.

—R. C. K.

ABOVE: Spocott Windmill.
BELOW: *Constellation* mast.

The gunboat *Philadelphia* is brought into the Smithsonian Institution by Jim Richardson. Part of an emergency fleet under command of Benedict Arnold, the *Philadelphia* was sunk while engaging the British fleet in Lake Champlain in October 1776. ABOVE: As it looked when raised in 1935. UPPER RIGHT: Protected by a wooden case, the vessel is brought into the Museum of Science and Technology while the building is under construction. LOWER RIGHT: As it looks today. Smithsonian Institution photos.

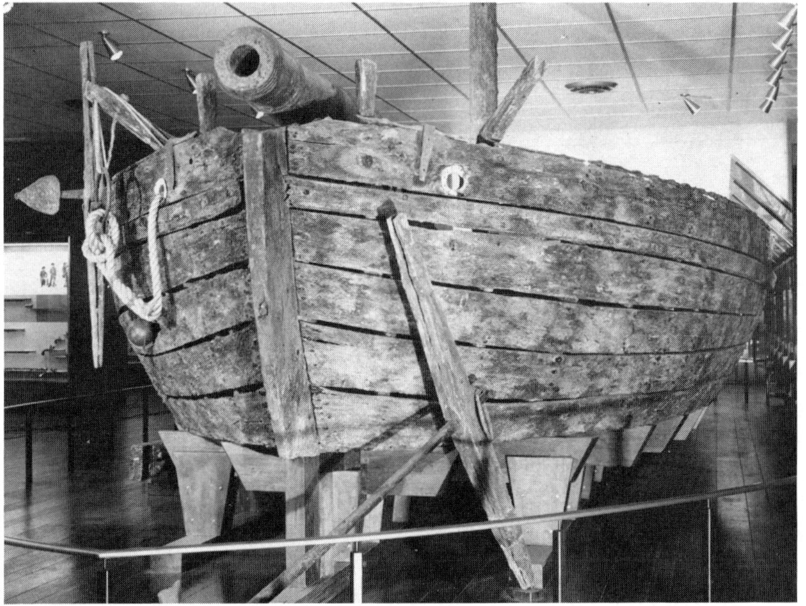

Maryland *Dove*. Photo by Michael Wootton.

Adventurer and *Dove* come together for film-making.

The *Jenny Norman*. LEFT: Launching sequence. ABOVE: Horn timber construction. BELOW: handcarved billet head. RIGHT: On the railway for for fresh bottom paint, prior to trying out the sails (August, 1985).

The Chesapeake Bay bugeye is distinguished by a round bilge, two masts, and leg-o'-mutton (triangular) sails. The bugeye is a direct descendent of the dugout, log canoe, and brogan, with borrowings from schooners and other vessels. The first bugeyes were built from logs and were double-enders. Some round and square stern versions were built, but this added greatly to the cost. A few bugeyes remain under sail; others have been converted to power, for use as "buyboats" to receive the oyster catch. Hard-chine boats have been built with bugeye-type rigs, but these would be called three-sail bateaux, not bugeyes. Other than the Jenny Norman, *no bugeye has been built on the Bay in many, many years.*

Appendix

Picking the Hull Form

The boat I chose for this book is a schooner. I wanted to use something that is fairly familiar to everyone, and I doubt it should be what I am building for myself, because somebody would say, "Well, he thinks the only boat in the world is a bugeye." I should think it ought to be a small schooner, about 40 feet. A schooner's construction is basic. If you can build a schooner you can build a sloop or any other *round-bilge* boat. Certainly if you can build a centerboarder you can build a keel boat. A centerboard well and all that stuff is one of the complicated things in a schooner—epecially if you have somebody design it. It's not so difficult if you work it out for yourself.

When I propose a schooner, I'm talking about a schooner hull and schooner sail rig. You have the same parts as a bugeye, you have the same procedures. Both are round-bilge boats, built with heavy frames. The only difference in the hull is that when you begin to get up above the deck you'd have *top timbers* and *caprails* and that sort of thing on a little schooner and in the bugeye you would not; you'd either have a round stern or a double-ender. The *Norman* is round stern. I did a round stern in preference to a double-ender because I wanted the room aft on her deck. Whenever anybody is out and has folks aboard, sooner or later the thrill of sitting there steering and all like that wanes, and it generally winds up that whoever is responsible is the one that has to sit there and handle the boat. I always thought it was lots more interesting to the person who has to handle the boat to have his guests within speak-

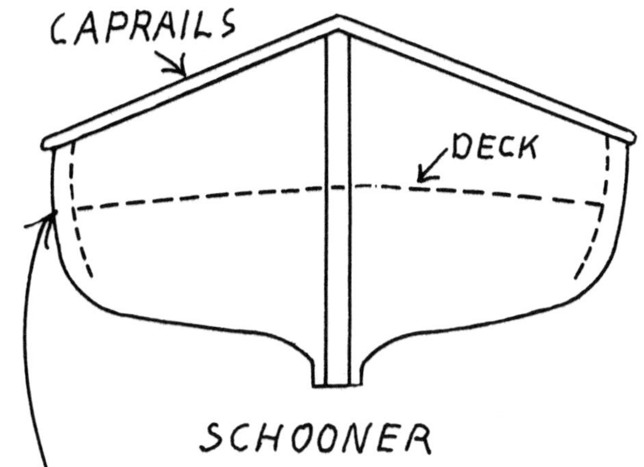

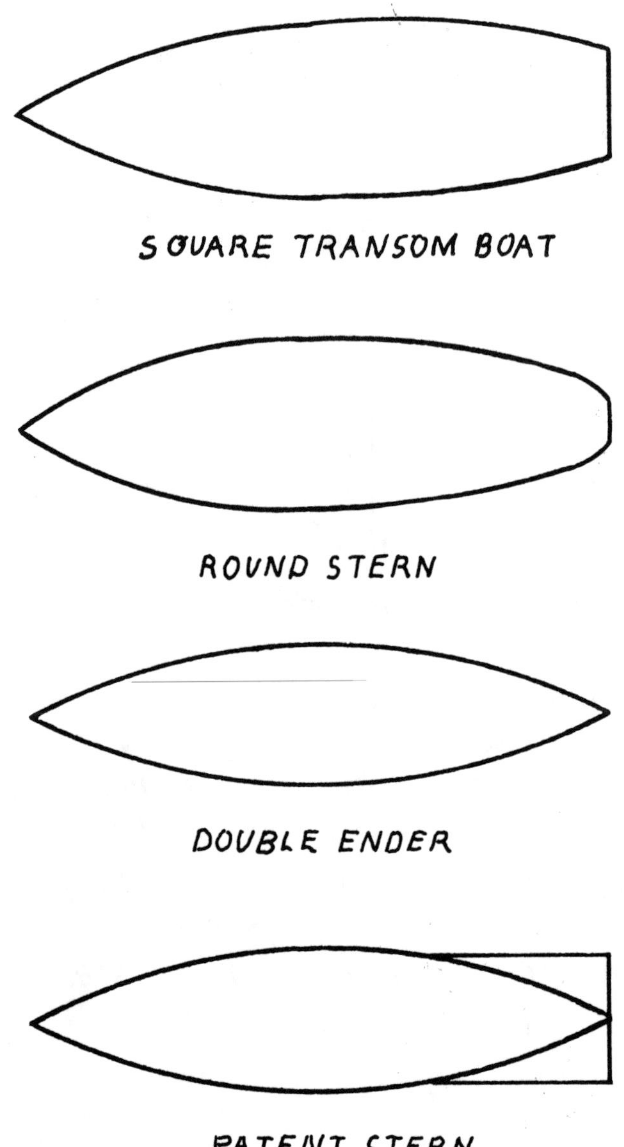

ing distance of him. With a double-ender you just are too crowded aft. You just don't have that much room. Some of them built a big platform out over the stern, called a *patent stern*. They did that so that they could carry a pushboat, hung from *davits*. I'll have davits too. I want to carry something or other, a small boat of some description. But I don't like a patent stern. It's ugly.

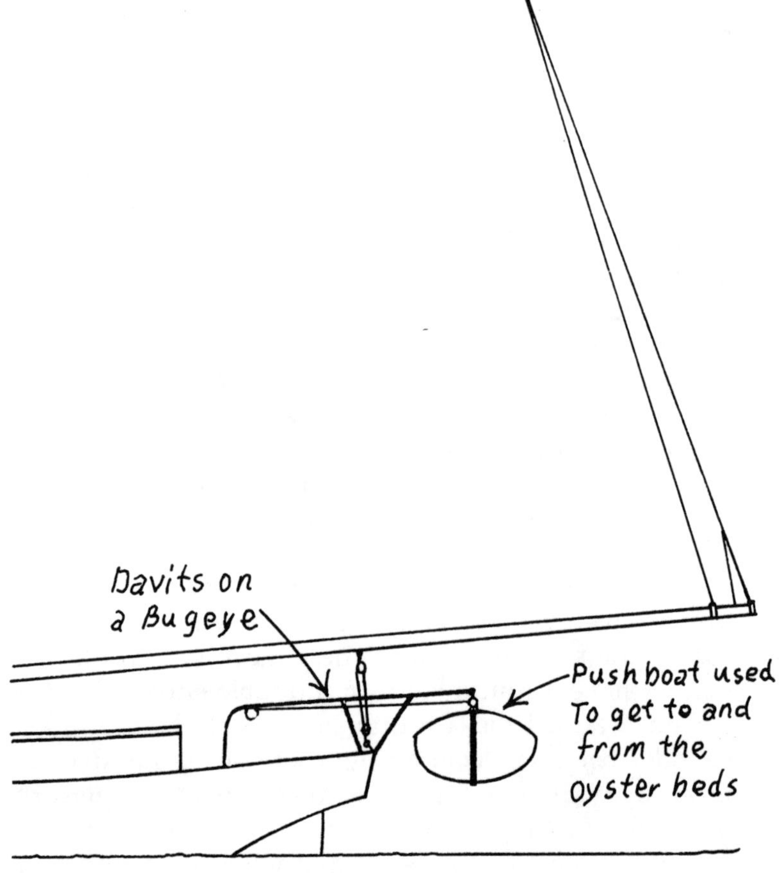

Centerboard vs. Deep Keel

When I was younger the deep keel boat was the only thing to have. If you were going offshore and didn't have a keel boat you just couldn't go. It didn't make any difference what Capt. Slocum* had done you still couldn't do it. You were also considered insane if you went out with anything other than a double-ender. I never have known how that got started unless the Vikings did a lot to promote it.

It is true that a centerboarder is not as safe and efficient as a deep keel boat because if you knock a centerboarder down and she picks herself back up again it is almost a miracle or an act of God or conditions that would be one in a thousand that would do that. A keel boat can do a complete 90 degree layover and still come up alive, providing her sails are down and everything else is set for rough weather. It is possible to knock a schooner down and in the next sea have her set herself back up again, even without a deep keel. But you can't expect that in a schooner. She'll spill her ballast sure as fate. Possibly, if you could hold her ballast under her ceiling and not have it dump into her cabin top she'd survive a half a roll.

A lot of our work boats, and even our old ships, had boxes of stones in them as ballast, and they emptied the boxes when they rolled over on their sides. What happened was that when they rolled they dumped the ballast that was in the upper side down in the lower side which was the last of the disaster.

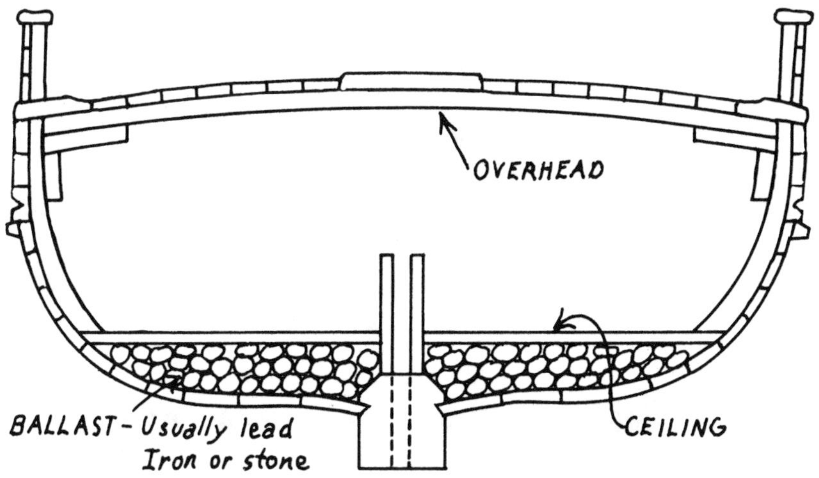

On a boat, the part you stand on, below deck, is called the ceiling and the area above you is called overhead. The ceiling is the second bottom. It is on top of the frames, and the ballast is generally underneath it. The ceiling is usually not fastened down sufficiently to hold the ballast if the boat rolls over.

*Capt. Joshua Slocum was the first to circumnavigate the globe single-handed, in a 35-foot shallow-draft sloop named *Spray*. He left Boston April 24, 1895, and returned three years later.

CENTERBOARDER
Board pivots at forward end-and can be hauled up in shallow water.

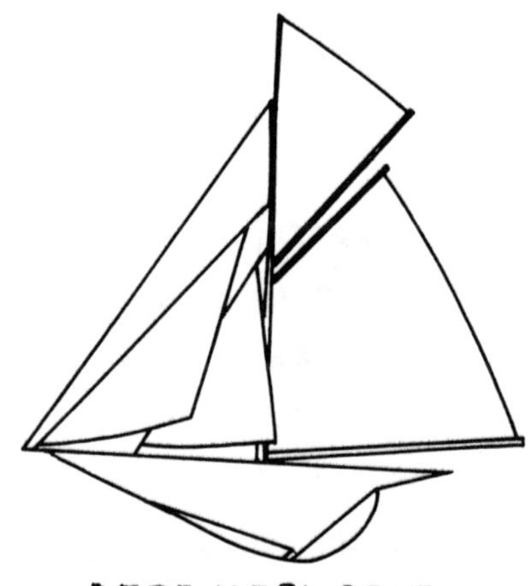

DEEP KEEL BOAT

LEE BOARDS

So deep keel boats are the safest. they're more expensive to build, and they're more expensive to go places in, because you have to go into the deep harbors and that's where everything costs the most. You can never gunkhole.* They're not much good for any place like the south side of Long Island Sound where there's a lot of shallow water. That's where we sold a lot of skipjacks, because they are shallow and can run into places. Here on the Bay, if you have a deep keel boat, unless you have local knowledge you pretty well stay out there in the Bay, and unless you just like to go up and down that's about all there is to it.

Our fathers and grandfathers went everywhere in centerboard boats. But then they were not yachtsmen so they didn't know it couldn't be done. Schooners out of Cambridge went all through the Bahamas and all down everywhere there in the tropical fruit trade, which was a layer of rum in the bottom of them and a layer of fruit on the top. They paid duty on the fruit and huckstered the rum, at tremendous profit. There was always a buyer in Baltimore who was ready to take it off some evening.

The Dutch have gotten really adept with leeboards, with some truly beautiful boats. Leeboards give you a shallow draft boat without the need to have a centerboard trunk in the middle of your quarters. They also save the keel from being all chopped up with a slot in it. But you can never single-hand a boat of any size with leeboards; it's just not something that one person can handle.

---

*Sailors' term for exploring small inlets.

Q. What influenced you to build a round-bilge boat, rather than a hard-chine boat like a skipjack or bateau? Round-bilge must take five or ten times longer to build?

Well, hard chine would take me as far as I want to go, and it doesn't make any difference what people say about round bilge being better offshore and that kind of thing. They're building more and more shrimpers all the time hard chine. And certainly if there's anybody who is out in the open it's the shrimper. So it's not a question of strength and stability and like that. But it's just like you get transportation from a Ford and you get transportation from a Cadillac. There's a little bit of clout with a round bilge that's hard to explain, unless you want to admit something. In building them, the biggest difference is in the amount of framing that goes into a round-bilge boat, compared to hard chine. It takes lots longer, of course, and is more expensive. But you're lots more comfortable in a round-bilge boat than in a hard chine for the most part. It would be very difficult to put that much money and time in a a hard chine and have her as nice as most round bilgers. You can just get a lot better hull form, more pleasing to the eye and all that sort of thing in a round bilge boat than in a hard chine.

Q. Let's get to the question of speed. Some people say that a round-bilge boat is faster than a hard-chine. Do you agree?

Well, we know that all the ocean racers, all of the J-boats, now all of the little K-boats, those people would turn over in their graves if somebody would come out with a hard-chine boat in competition. But it's always been an intriguing thing to me. I wish somebody would design a boat with a double chine, that would heel over in two stages, and see how she did with those polished aluminum and copper jobs sailing now. I'm talking about the ones that sail for the America's cup, which are supposed to be the last

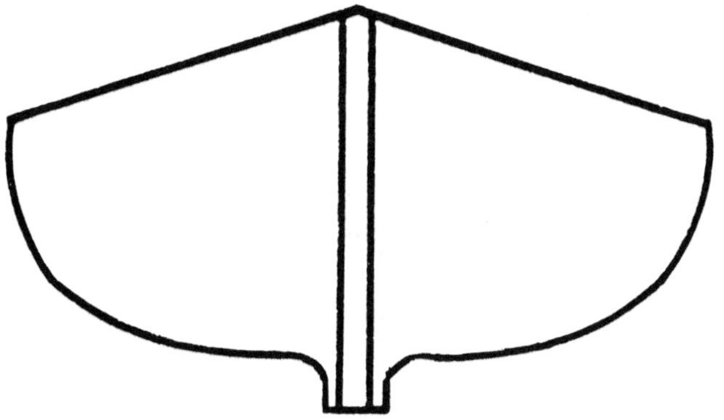

ROUND-BILGE BOAT
The hull is curved, requires lots of framing

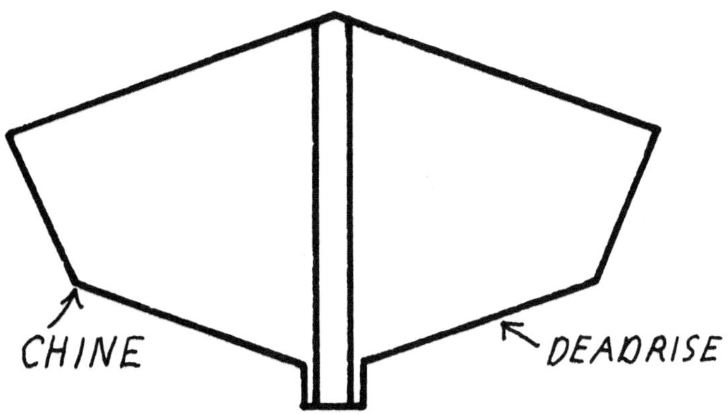

HARD-CHINE BOAT
Sides and bottom are straight. Requires very little framing.

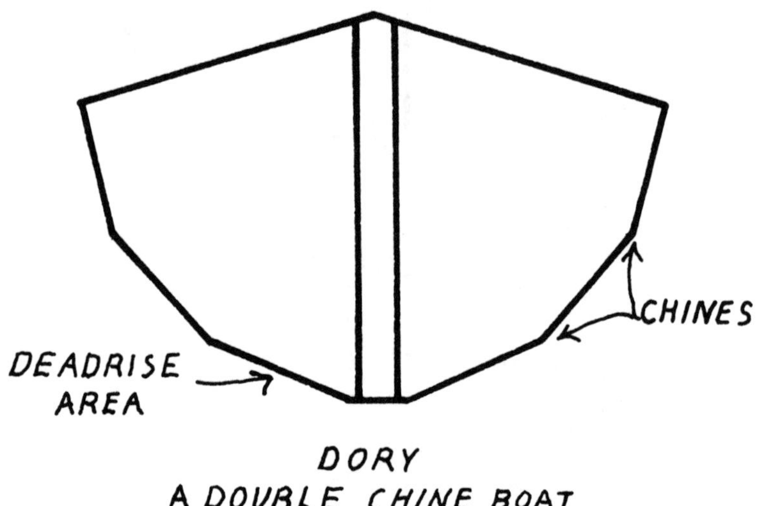

DORY
A DOUBLE CHINE BOAT

word in design and sophistication there is anywhere. I mean if there is a hot designer anywhere in the world these people will go for him. But the designers all do the same, of course. A lot of them blow it, too.

Q.Have you ever seen a double chine boat?

Sure. We've got double chine in *dories*. It comes up with *deadrise,* then there's a chine, then the next chine, and then the sides. I know there's no hard edges on a whale. I know that. But I'm just wondering if it would make a great deal of difference. In the *log canoes,* they do everything they can to keep them from having a sharp edge. Even their worm shoe and everything is rounded on its corners. They just can't abide a sharp corner. But I'm not too sure that round corners are what did it as much as finally, they began to get the skipper, the crew and the boat to agree with each other and then they began to do something with it. I have a friend who's had his boat for 11 years now, and he says, "We're beginning to be close enough to see who wins." So, by and by, you get to the place where you're in there. In the meantime, he's rounding all his edges. I'm just wondering if he let his edges be sharp and just stayed with it, if he wouldn't still be close enough to see who won.

Q. What determines the speed of a hull?

Well, wetted surface used to be the great idea, you know, to do away with as much wetted surface as you could, because that's friction. But you know you can't have a boat stand up and carry sail unless you have some wetted surface. You also know that if you're going to race it, by and by you're going to be out there when it's blowing, and all you're going to be is knocked down if you don't have wetted surface. So, what they've been trying to do in the little 12s is to reach some kind of happy medium, and

CHESAPEAKE LOG CANOE

Originally built from hollowed logs then from logs held together by iron rods.

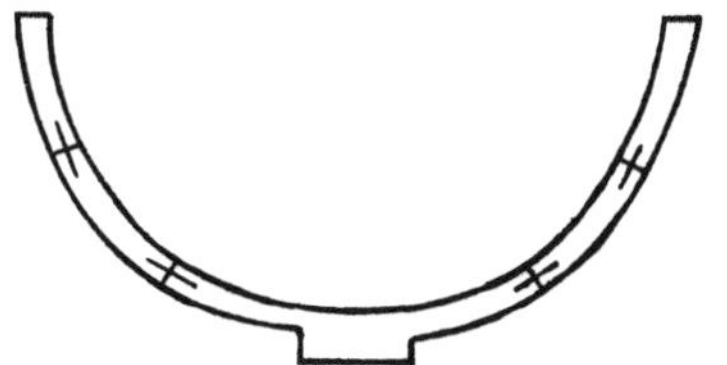

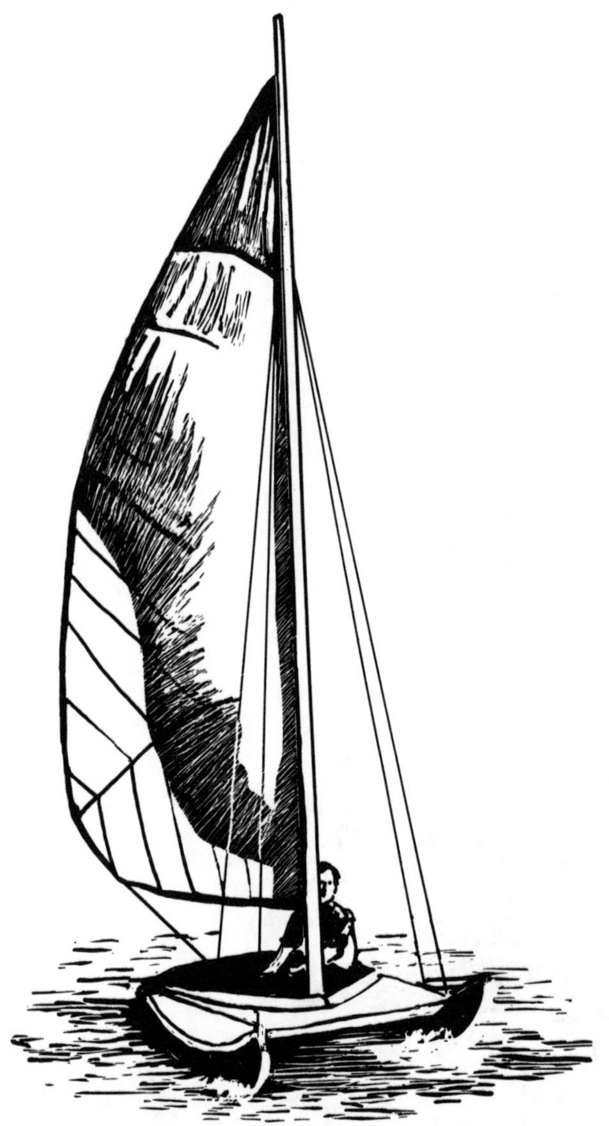

DOUBLE HULL CATAMARAN

These are the fastest sailing boats. The twin hulls provide stability with the least amount wetted surface in relation to sail area carried.

they've gone back and forth with centerboard contours, with rudder contours, every other kind of contour, blunt bows, full bows, same at the stern.

Q. But that's all within a certain size or class. Won't a larger sailboat go faster than a small sailboat?

Right. The speed is directly related to the size, all the more so with multi-hulls like the *catamarans.* It's theorized, and computerized, all like that, if you were of a mind to you could build a catamaran big enough to go 60 miles an hour.

The engineers calculate that if you scale a 20-foot boat up to 40 feet in direct proportion, it will go something like half again as fast, other things being equal, like the wind. According to these experts, the reason a big boat goes faster than a small boat has to do with the effort used up in making the bow wave. You have to push that water out of your way whether you are a long boat or a short boat. They say the bigger boat uses a smaller percentage of its energy in cutting the bow wave, so it is able to go faster. There are a lot of things involved here that aren't obvious, but certainly the result has proved true.

A small sailboat, say a 30-footer, will go maybe four to eight knots, depending on the wind and so forth. The original *Norma* is supposed to have run 14 miles an hour for eight consecutive hours with 40 tons of coal in her. She was 75-78 feet, something like that, which is a large bugeye. The Baltimore Clippers clocked nearly 20 knots on steady runs. They were 110-120 feet. But when they talk about the clipper and her speed and all like that, it's just alongside the yachts they're building nowadays. It's not so fast so far as a lot of boats that were never documented.

Of course it depends on whether you have speed in mind when the boat's being built. There were big boats on

BALTIMORE CLIPPER

the Bay called *rams* that weren't fast. They were strictly cargo carriers, big and bulky. They were not made for quick trips like the China trade. It's a question of balancing your needs.

Q. When people speak of a boat having "fine" lines what does that mean?

Long and slim. Nothing abrupt. Some of the log canoes had almost clipper ship lines. That's the reason they were as fast as they were.

Q. Do graceful lines always serve a function, or is it also a matter of looks?

Well, you can make a boat attractive or ugly. Sometimes an ugly boat is rather fast. But you know what old man Nate Herreschoff said. He said a pretty boat is like a pretty woman. Everybody thinks that she'll be fast even if she isn't.

CHESAPEAKE BAY RAM

Advantages of Size

Scaling up or down is something you do often in boat building—for instance in going from a test model to full size, or when you use the lines of a successful boat to build another boat larger or smaller.

All sorts of strange things happen when you scale a boat up or down in size. According to the engineers and physicists, as you increase the length by some factor, you would take that same factor and square it to get your sail area and wetted surface, cube it to get your weight and displacement, and improve your stability to the fourth power. In other words, if you take the lines off a 30-footer and build a 60-foot boat to the exact same proportions, the 60-foot boat will be twice the length, but will have four times more sail area and wetted surface, will be eight times heavier and roomier, and 16 times more stable.

The 60-foot boat would go nearly half again as fast as the 30-foot boat under a formula that says the speed of any given design will increase at the same rate as the square root of the waterline length. The reason for the speed difference is that the effort to start the wave rolling away from the bow is not all that much greater for the big boat than for the small boat. The big boat has relatively more energy left over to overcome friction and therefore it moves faster.

These things have been worked out over the years by people connected with the English and American navies—William Froude and Admiral David Taylor in particular.

Glossary

BALLAST—Weight carried low in hull to keep boat from tipping over. (65)

BATTEN—A long, thin, flexible piece of wood. (32, 33, 37)

BEAD—Decorative groove running the length of the boat below the sheerline. (21, 35)

BEAM—Width of a boat at its widest point. (xi)

BILGE—The lowest area inside the boat, below the waterline. (xi, 35)

BOB CHAINS—Chains that tie the head stay and jib stay to the hull of the boat. (29, 72)

BOOM—Horizontal pole that holds the foot of a sail. (4, 70, 78)

BOW—Front end of the boat. (xi)

BOWSPRIT—Spar at front of boat for carrying headsails. (4, 49)

BREAST HOOK—Piece at bow which ties sheer planks together. (29)

BRIGHT WORK—Wood varnished to show natural grain. (63)

BUGEYE—Three sailed Chesapeake Bay workboat with round bilge, originally made from logs. (94)

CABIN—The enclosed area where passengers sleep and eat. (xi, 50-59)

CANT FRAMES—Frames that come up from keel at an angle. (33)

CEILING—Inner hull, inside covering of ribs. (41, 59, 97)

CATAMARAN—Fast twin-hulled boat. (103)

CENTER OF EFFORT—Point on sail where principal wind forces are directed. (10, 11)

CENTER OF LATERAL RESISTANCE—Point on boat which offers greatest resistance to being pushed sideways by wind. (10, 11)

CENTERBOARD—Flat piece, pivoting at forward end, which can be lowered below the hull to retard side slippage when boat is sailing to windward. (xi, 28, 29)

CENTERBOARD WELL (or TRUNK)—Waterproof enclosure atop slot in keel, into which centerboard can be drawn when not in use. (xi, 28, 29)

CHINE—Where bottom and sides meet (99, 100)

CLEW—Lower back corner of sail. (83)

CLAMPS—Long pieces that tie tops of ribs together below the deckline. (34)

COCKPIT—Open area where the boat is steered and principal sails are controlled. (xi)

COUNTER—Underside of transom. (36)

DAVITS—Deck cranes used to haul tenders and other small auxiliary boats. (96)

DEADEYES—Hard round wooden blocks through which lanyards are strung to maintain tension on shrouds. (74, 75)

DEADRISE—The rise of the hull from keel to waterline. (21)

DEADWOOD—Filler pieces used between hull and rudder. (27)

DECK HOUSE—Structure that encloses the cabin. (xi, 54, 55)

DECKING—Top covering of the hull. (xi, 40-47)

DOPHIN STRIKER (or MARTINGALE)—Pole pointing downward under bowsprit, helping to support outer headsails. (73)

DOWNHAUL—Line used to bring a sail down. (78, 79)

DRAFT—Depth of hull in water. (xi)

FLARE—Contour of bow above the waterline. (21)

FLOOR—Framing member which rests on the keel. (30)

FRAMES (or RIBS)—Vertical pieces which come up from the keel and determine the shape of the hull. (xi, 3034, 37)

FREEBOARD—Area of hull above waterline.

FUTTOCKS—Pieces which are joined together to form the ribs. (30)

GAFF—Pole carrying top of rectangular sail. (4, 7-9)

GARBOARD—Lowest plank, next to keel or keelson. (27)

GARBOARD STRAKE—Bottommost line of planking. (35)

HALYARD—Line used to raise a sail. (78, 79)

HELM—Steering station, tiller or wheel. (xi)

HORN TIMBER—Framing piece at back end of boat, supporting the hull area aft of the sternpost. (xi, 25, 29)

HOUNDS—Hollowed area near top of mast where supporting rigging attaches. (72, 73)

KEEL—Backbone of the boat; the heavy framing piece to which everything else attaches. (xi, 26, 97)

KEELSON—Like a keel, except that it is coverd by frames and planking so that it does not protrude down into the water. (26)

KNEE—Strengthening piece, using natural curve of grain. (25)

KNIGHTHEADS—Vertical pieces that provide an additional place to fasten planking aft of the stem. They protrude above deck. (29, 34, 35)

LONGHEAD (GAMMON KNEE)—Gracefully curved piece under the bowsprit. (27)

LANYARD—Short line used for lashing or securing. (75)

LAZARETTE—Storage area at stern of boat. (52, 53)

LAZY JACKS—Lines rigged to cradle sails when they are lowered. (73)

LOG CANOE—Swift Chesapeake Bay sailing craft built from logs. (101)

MAST—Upright pole that holds the sails. (4, 66, 69)

OUTHAUL—Line used to make foot of sail taut. (79, 83)

PARCEL—Wrap wire with canvas. (74, 76)

PLANKING—The covering on the sides of a wooden boat; the "skin" over the ribs. (27, 35-39)

PORT—Left side of the boat. (xi)

PUNGY—Chesapeake Bay schooner used for oystering in 1800s. (62)

RAM—Straight-sided Chesapeake Bay cargo schooner. (104)

REEF (v.)—Reduce sail area by bundling and tying off lower sections of the sail. (14, 15)

RIBS—See FRAMES.

RUDDER—Large flat piece at rear of hull which pivots in water to determine direction of boat's movement. Controlled by tiller or wheel. (xi, 48)

SAMSON POST—Heavy duty bit on foredeck for holding anchor or dock lines. (47)

SCHOONER—Multimasted sailing vessel with largest sail aft. (8, 9, 95, 103, 104)

SEIZE—Bind with soft wire. (74, 76)

SERVE—Cover with marline. (74, 76)

SHEER—Rake of the deck fore and aft. (21)

SHEER STRAKE—Topmost line of planking. (35)

SHEET—Line used to trim sail in relation to the wind. (78, 79, 80)

SHELVES—Horizontal pieces that lay atop clamps on larger vessels. (34)

SHROUDS—Wire or rope stays that run up from the sides of a boat to support the mast. (72, 73)

SHUTTER STRAKE—Last line of planking installed. (35)

SKIPJACK—Two-sail, hard-chine Chesapeake Bay workboat, used to dredge oysters. (12-14, 18)

SPILING—Transferring measurements from a rounded hull to a flat board. (37)

STARBOARD—Right side of boat. (xi)

STEM—Framing piece at front end of boat. (xi, 29, 35)

STERN—Back end of the boat. (xi)

STERNPOST—Framing piece at back end of boat, coming up from the keel. (25, 29)

STIFF—Holds steady in puffy wind. (14, 15)

STRAKE—A line of planking running from bow to stern. (35)

TACK—Lower front corner of sail. (82) Also, maneuver of boat when sailing to windward.

TEACLE—Extra block and fall to help lift sail or anchor. (81)

TENDER—Sensitive to wind changes. Also, a small auxiliary boat. (15)

TILLER—Inboard steering stick which attaches directly to rudder post. (xi, 48)

TOPPING LIFT—A line from top of mast to outer end of boom, preventing boom from dropping on deck when sails are lowered. (72, 73)

TRANSOM—Flat section at the stern, where the nameboard goes. (25)

TRAVELER—Metal rod on which sheet block rides when boat shifts from one tack to another. (80)

TRESTLE TREE—Rigging support near top of mast. (74, 78)

TRIATIC STAY—Wire tying foremast to mainmast. (72, 73)

TUMBLEHOME—Where the hull turns inward above the waterline. (21)

WHEEL—Spoked steering unit which controls rudder with aid of gears. (xi, 48)

WORM SHOE—Flat piece at bottom of keel. (3)